Dynamite Résumés

Books and CD-ROMs by Drs. Ron and Caryl Krannich

101 Dynamite Answers to Interview Questions
101 Secrets of Highly Effective Speakers
201 Dynamite Job Search Letters
Best Jobs For the 21st Century
Change Your Job, Change Your Life
The Complete Guide to International Jobs and Careers
The Complete Guide to Public Employment
The Directory of Federal Jobs and Employers
Discover the Best Jobs For You!
Dynamite Cover Letters
Dynamite Networking For Dynamite Jobs
Dynamite Résumés
Dynamite Salary Negotiations
Dynamite Tele-Search
The Educator's Guide to Alternative Jobs and Careers
Find a Federal Job Fast!
From Air Force Blue to Corporate Gray
From Army Green to Corporate Gray
From Navy Blue to Corporate Gray
Get a Raise in 7 Days
High Impact Résumés and Letters
International Jobs Directory
Interview For Success
Job-Power Source CD-ROM
Jobs and Careers With Nonprofit Organizations
Jobs For People Who Love Travel
Mayors and Managers
Moving Out of Education
Moving Out of Government
The Politics of Family Planning Policy
Re-Careering in Turbulent Times
Résumés and Job Search Letters For Transitioning Military Personnel
Shopping and Traveling in Exotic Asia
Shopping in Exciting Australia and Papua New Guinea
Shopping in Exotic Places
Shopping the Exotic South Pacific
Treasures and Pleasures of Australia
Treasures and Pleasures of China
Treasures and Pleasures of Hong Kong
Treasures and Pleasures of India
Treasures and Pleasures of Indonesia
Treasures and Pleasures of Italy
Treasures and Pleasures of Paris and the French Riviera
Treasures and Pleasures of Singapore and Malaysia
Treasures and Pleasures of Thailand
Ultimate Job Source CD-ROM

Dynamite Résumés
101 Great Examples and Tips For Success

Fourth Edition

Ronald L. Krannich, Ph.D.
Caryl Rae Krannich, Ph.D.

IMPACT PUBLICATIONS
Manassas Park, VA

DYNAMITE RÉSUMÉS: 101 Great Examples And Tips For Success!

Fourth Edition

Library of Congress Cataloging-in-Publication Data

Krannich, Ronald L.
    Dynamite résumés: 101 great examples and tips for success! / Ronald L. Krannich, Caryl Rae Krannich.—4th. ed.
      p. cm.
    Includes bibliographical references and index.
    ISBN 1-57023-100-1
    1. Résumés (Employment) I. Krannich, Caryl Rae. II. Title.
HF5383.K69   1999
808'.06665—dc20   98-46203
                                            CIP

Publisher: For information on Impact Publications, including current and forthcoming publications, authors, press kits, bookstore, and submission requirements, visit Impact's Web site: *www.impactpublications.com*

Publicity/Rights: For information on publicity, author interviews, and subsidiary rights, contact the Public Relations and Marketing Department: Tel. 703/361-7300 or Fax 703/335-9486.

Sales/Distribution: All bookstore sales are handled through Impact's trade distributor: National Book Network, 15200 NBN Way, Blue Ridge Summit, PA 17214, Tel. 1-800-462-6420. All other sales and distribution inquiries should be directed to the publisher: Sales Department, IMPACT PUBLICATIONS, 9104-N Manassas Dr., Manassas Park, VA 20111-5211, Tel. 703/361-7300, Fax 703/335-9486, or E-mail: *resume@impactpublications.com*

Contents

v

CHAPTER 6: Dynamite Résumé Sampler 116

CHAPTER 7: Using Electronic Résumés and Databases in the New Job Market 142

Preface

Writing and distributing résumés in response to job vacancies has been a time-honored tradition for decades. While some people have never had to write a résumé—because they completed application forms or were hired on the basis of an interview alone—more and more individuals must write résumés today. From blue collar workers to white collar professionals, résumés are an accepted and preferred medium for communicating one's qualifications to employers. Even prospective federal government employees, who prior to 1995 were required to complete a highly structured application form (the much dreaded SF-171), can now submit résumés in response to federal vacancy announcements.

Contrary to what you may have heard from others, résumés are here to stay, and in a very big way. As the job market becomes more competitive, as employers seek highly skilled and experienced individuals, and as new technology becomes increasingly applied to the candidate selection process, résumés are playing a much greater role in the employment process than ever before. At the same time, the structure and content of résumés have changed in light of new employer expectations. No longer are "summary of work history" résumés designed for the 1970s and 1980s appropriate for today's job market. Employers expect résumés to tell them about an individual's relevant "patterns of performance" and how he or she will "add value" to the employer's organization. Consequently, the *language of résumés* has changed from historical information and statements of formal duties and responsibilities to the use of action verbs and nouns that form coherent statements of motivated abilities and patterns of accomplishments. In other words, today's résumés must be *employer-centered*—tell employers what you have done, can do, and will most likely do for them once you come on their payroll. The increasing use of technology (optical scanners) to scan résumés for keywords means more and more applicants need to develop an effective electronic version of their résumé so it can be "read" by computers. As employers increasingly use the Internet to recruit candidates, more and more job seekers will need to develop e-mail versions of their résumés as well as learn how to conduct an online job search.

Recognizing the increasing importance of résumés and sensitive to the expectations of employers, this new edition of *Dynamite Résumés* outlines the major principles for writing, producing, distributing, and following-up résumés in today's highly competitive job market. Unlike many other résumé guides that primarily focus on the writing process or are essentially compilations of résumé examples, this book focuses on what's really important when communicating qualifications to employers. We focus on the whole process that produces results for both job applicants and employers. Writing according to principles of good résumé writing is only one of many elements that results in desired outcomes. The other three involve résumé production, distribution, and follow-up. Failure to closely link these three additional processes to the résumé writing process often means a well-written résumé never achieves its true potential. Indeed, the best written résumés are only as good as the quality of their production, distribution, and follow-up. Neglect any one of these processes and you may effectively kill your résumé.

As you navigate today's job market, make sure you pay particular attention to how you can best distribute and follow-up your résumé. The good news is that you now have more opportunities to distribute your résumé given the increasing use of résumé databases and career services available on the Internet. In Chapter 7 we identify several of these new opportunities as well as many of the key resources available to help you navigate this new and rapidly developing electronic job market.

Whatever you do, make sure you approach today's job market with a dynamite résumé that is written, produced, distributed, and followed-up according to the many principles outlined in this book. Use our internal and external evaluation forms in Chapter 4 to assess how well your résumé meets the expectations of today's employers. Most important of all, follow-up, follow-up, follow-up. Writing, producing, and distributing a dynamite résumé without proper and persistent follow-up is a waste of time. If you're going to write it right, follow it up frequently. If you observe this simple follow-up rule, you'll be amazed with the results. You'll indeed put dynamite into your résumé.

Ronald L. Krannich
Caryl Rae Krannich

Dynamite Résumés

Welcome to the New World of Résumés

A lot of changes have taken place in the job market during the past few years. While companies continue to downsize, they also face labor shortages in a new booming, talent-driven economy. In 1998, one of the biggest problems facing employers was how to best recruit and retain top talent to better manage company growth. At the same time, one of the biggest problems for job seekers was how to best identify the perfect employer who would offer them a rewarding job.

Connecting in the Right Places

The age-old problem of how to connect the right employer with the right candidate has increasingly moved from print to electronic mediums as the Internet now plays an important role in the job search and hiring processes. Indeed, by 1998 more and more employers and candidates had learned an important lesson—top talent tends to congregate in the digital job market that operates via the Internet. If you're not using the Internet to recruit (employer) or identify employers and jobs (candidate), you're not fully utilizing today's most important employment resources. You may be missing the right places for finding jobs or acquiring top talent.

While the job search has increasingly turned digital, the traditional one- and two-page résumé continues to play a critical role in the employment process. Communication mediums have changed—moving from the traditional print classified ad and mailed résumé to faxes, e-mail, databases, and Web sites—but the message remains the same for job seekers: clearly communicate their qualifications to employers. For employers, resumes remain the most efficient and effective means of screening candidates for job interviews. If as a job seeker you neglect your résumé, you may well miss out on some terrific job opportunities in today's job market.

A Job Market Requiring Dynamite Résumés

Today's new job market is especially responsive to dynamite résumés. These résumés are designed for a re-engineered work world that operates in a highly competitive 21st century economy. These résumés are read by seasoned employers as well as scanned by new search and retrieval software and transmitted via e-mail. Indeed, you'll need a dynamite résumé to be successful in this job market. Without such a résumé—complete with the latest bells, whistles, and buzz words—you are likely to flounder in the newly evolving job market that is redefining the way most people will find jobs in the 21st century.

❑ **Today's new job market requires dynamite résumés.**

❑ **The new job search revolution requires that your résumé speak to both employers and electronic scanning technology.**

❑ **The application of new technology to the hiring process means résumés are playing an increasingly important role in the job search.**

❑ **Contrary to what many people believed only a few years ago, résumés are here to stay, and in a very big way.**

Our best advice for today: You may want to throw away your old résumé which may be designed for a different era or a traditional job market which is becoming obsolete. Start fresh with a dynamite résumé designed for today's new job market.

The rules and mediums for finding jobs, communicating qualifications to employers, and screening candidates are rapidly changing. No longer do you just type a résumé and send it in the mail to an employer. As technology becomes increasingly used in the employment process, most résumé guides using the type-and-mail approach have become outdated. This revolution has important implications on how you should write, distribute, and follow-up your résumé in today's job market. It requires you to write a résumé that speaks to employers through both paper and electronic mediums. Your résumé must be readable by both human beings and the latest résumé scanning technology. It also must be designed so it can be accessed through electronic databases, posted on electronic bulletin boards, and be transmitted in cyberspace via e-mail. Above all, your résumé must grab the attention of employers who will want to invite you to a job interview.

Does Your Résumé Speak the Right Language?

Large corporations continue to downsize, permanently laying off thousands of redundant workers each week. At the same time, many of these same companies have difficulty hiring people with the right skills required for their newly restructured operations. Government policies increasingly shift toward creating jobs, retraining workers, and promoting one-stop job centers. Even the federal government's application process is shifting toward greater use of the Internet, resumes, and new automated applications for screening candidates.

From the perspective of job seekers, today's job finding process—from electronic bulletin boards displaying vacancy announcements to résumé databases linking candidates to employers—is undergoing numerous changes centered on the role of résumés. From the perspective of employers, the recruitment and screening processes are finally becoming more scientific, systematic, and predictable. All of these changes point in one direction—the increasingly powerful role résumés play in the employment process, from locating employers and screening candidates to conducting job interviews.

These momentous changes are enhancing the role of résumés in the job search. If you believed paperless offices would result from the computer revolution, then you might have believed in the coming demise of résumés. We, of course, now know the computer revolution had just the opposite effect— dramatically increased the volume of office paper. So, too, will be a similar fate for résumés—the newly evolving job market will place even greater emphasis on using résumés for finding employment and screening candidates.

Contrary to what many people believed only a few years ago, résumés are here to stay, and in a very big way. Application of new technology to the job search means you simply must write dynamite résumés tailored to the needs of specific employers. You must pay particular attention to the **language** you incorporate in your résumé. Carefully selecting a "keyword" language sensitive to optical scanners becomes one of the most important considerations in writing résumés for today's job market.

Unknown to many job seekers, résumés are playing an increasingly central role in the job finding process. If you want to get a good job in today's job market, your résumé simply must be first-class; it should incorporate the major principles found throughout this book. Therefore, you should spend a disproportionate amount of time crafting the very best résumé possible.

If you've not already created a dynamite résumé, let's spend a few hours sharing some of the inside secrets of writing and distributing some of the most powerful communications for affecting today's rapidly changing job market.

You Can Do Better

When did you last write a dynamite résumé? How important was the selection of language to summarize your experience? How well did you write, produce, distribute, and follow-up your résumé? Who evaluated it and how? Did it immediately grab the attention of employers who called you for interviews? Would it also do well in the face of today's electronic scanning technology? How well did it stand out from the crowd of other résumés? Did it clearly communicate your qualifications and future performance to potential employers? What did it really say about you as both a professional and a person? Did it become your ticket to interviews or did it dash your job search expectations?

Regardless of what resulted from your previous résumé efforts, let's turn to your future success which should include dynamite résumés.

Abused and Misused Communication

Résumés are some of the most abused and misused forms of job search communication. Not knowing how to best communicate their qualifications to employers, many job seekers go through the ritual of writing uninspired documents that primarily document their work history rather than provide evidence for predicting their future performance and potential value to employers. Lacking a clear sense of purpose, they fail to properly connect their résumé writing activities to their larger job search tasks. Rather than communicate their future performance and potential value to employers, they choose to document their past employment history which may or may not be relevant to employers' immediate and future needs.

> Dynamite résumés grab the attention of potential employers who, in turn, invite you to job interviews.

But writing a résumé is really the easiest thing to do. Once completing the writing and producing it, many job seekers don't know how to best manage their résumé in relation to potential employers. Most just send it in the mail, as if job interviews and offers are primarily a function of increased direct-mail activity. Preoccupied with the magic of writing right, few job seekers engage in effective résumé **distribution and follow-up** activities—the keys for getting your résumé read and responded to. Instead, they circulate a lot of pretty paper that often goes to all the wrong people and all the wrong places!

You can do better than most job seekers if you produce dynamite résumés. Unlike other résumés, dynamite résumés are designed with the larger job search in mind—they grab the attention of potential employers who, in turn, invite you to job interviews. You conduct dynamite interviews because your answers and questions are consistent with your résumé. Your dynamite résumé should:

➤ Clearly communicate a sense of purpose, value, professionalism, competence, honesty, enthusiasm, and likability.

➤ Consistently observe the rules of good résumé writing—structure, form, grammar, word selection, categories, punctuation, spelling, inclusion/exclusion, length, and graphic design.

➤ Specifically link your interests, skills, abilities, and experience to the employer's present and future needs.

➤ Be produced in a professional manner, from paper stock to ink, to further communicate your professional image.

➤ Include the right combination of "keywords" used by search and retrieval software for scanning résumés electronically.

➤ Get distributed through the proper channels—mail, fax, and e-mail—and delivered into the hands of the right people—those who make the hiring decision.

➤ Regularly get followed-up with telephone calls, letters, and interviews.

➤ Stand out from the crowd by clearly speaking to employers—*"Let's interview this candidate who appears to have what we need."*

Unlike many other résumé books, which are primarily preoccupied with presenting proper résumé form and content on paper, or presenting numerous examples of résumés, *Dynamite Résumés* focuses on the whole communication process, from producing an outstanding written document (form, content, and production elements) to distributing and following-up your résumé with maximum impact. We focus on creating résumés that generate concrete **outcomes**—job interviews and offers.

A 30-Second Image Management Activity

Résumé writing is first and foremost a 30-second image management activity designed to motivate an employer to take action that results in you being invited to a job interview. After all, it takes employers no more than 30 seconds to read and respond to your résumé. If it is scanned and processed electronically, it takes only seconds for the computer software to match keywords on your résumé to determine whether or not your résumé should be selected for initial human consideration. Therefore, you must quickly **motivate** the reader to take action. Your résumé must communicate your best professional image in writing **before** you can expect to be invited to a job interview. How and what you write, as well as which methods you choose to disseminate and follow-up your message, will largely determine how effective you are in moving the employer to take action in reference to your qualifications.

❏ **Distribution and follow-up activities are the keys for getting your résumé read and responded to.**

❏ **Dynamite résumés are designed with the larger job search in mind.**

❏ **You should design a résumé that focuses on desired outcomes—it should generate job interviews and offers.**

❏ **Most employers spend no more than 30 seconds reading and responding to a résumé.**

❏ **To strangers reading your résumé, you essentially are what you write.**

Keep in mind that most employers are busy people who must make quick judgments about you based upon your written message. Within only 30 seconds, your written communication must motivate the reader to either select you in or take you out of consideration for a job interview. Neglect the importance of a 30-second dynamite résumé and you will surely neglect one of the most important elements in a successful job search. Your résumé will join the graveyard of so many other ineffective résumés.

You Are What You Write

When writing and sending résumés to strangers, you essentially are what you write. Your one- to two-page résumé succinctly says a great deal about your professionalism, competence, and personality that goes beyond just documenting your work history, experience, and education. Your résumé must have sufficient impact to move employers to contact you, interview you over the telephone, and hopefully invite you to a job interview that leads to a job offer and renewed career success. If you fail to properly write, produce, market, and follow-up your résumé, you will most likely conduct an ineffective job search.

Résumés Ready Do Count

Finding employment in today's job market poses numerous challenges for individuals who seek quality jobs that lead to good salaries, career advancement, and job security. The whole job finding process is chaotic, confusing, and frustrating. It requires a certain level of organization and communication skills aimed at identifying, contacting, and communicating your qualifications to potential employers. If you want to make this process best work for you, you must do more than just mail résumés in response to vacancy announcements.

To be most successful in finding employment, you should develop a plan of action that involves these seven distinct yet interrelated job search steps:

1. Assess your skills
2. Develop a job/career objective
3. Conduct research on employers and organizations
4. Write résumés and letters
5. Network for information, advice, and referrals
6. Interview for jobs
7. Negotiate salary and terms of employment

As illustrated on page 8, each of these steps represents important **communication skills** involving you in contact with others. Assessing your skills (Step 1), for example, requires conducting a systematic assessment of what you do well and enjoy doing—your strengths or motivated abilities and skills (MAS) that become translated into your "qualifications" for employers. Conducting research on individuals, organizations, communities, and jobs (Step 4) requires the use of investigative skills commonly associated with library research. Networking and interviewing (Steps 5-6) primarily involve the use of conversational skills—small talk and structured question/answer dialogues—by telephone and in face-to-face encounters.

But it is the critical résumé and letter writing step (4) that becomes the major communication challenge for most job seekers. Without strong writing skills, your job search is likely to flounder. Indeed, your ability to write dynamite

Job Search Steps and Stages

Box	Step	Stage
Identify motivated skills and abilities	1	
Specify a job/career objective	2	INVESTIGATIVE STAGE
Research individuals, organizations, communities, and jobs	3	
Produce résumés and job search letters	4	WRITING STAGE
Conduct informational/ networking interviews	5	
Manage job interviews	6	EMPLOYER CONTACT STAGE
Negotiate salary and terms of employment	7	

résumés and cover letters largely determines how quickly you will transform your job search from the investigative stage (research) to employer contact stages (networking, interviewing, salary negotiations). Your writing skills become the key element in moving your job search from the investigative stage to the final job offer stage. Writing demonstrates your competence.

In the job search, paper is the great equalizer. Most employers want to first see you on paper before meeting you in person. You along with many others must pass the written test **before** you can be considered for the face-to-face oral test. Whether you like it or not, you must put your professionalism, competence, and personality in writing before you can be taken seriously for a job interview. Thus, your writing activities may well become the most critical **transformation step** in your job search. Your writing skills become your ticket to job interviews that lead to job offers and employment.

For some reason, job search writing skills usually receive little attention beyond the perfunctory *"you must write a résumé and cover letter"* advisory. They also get dismissed as unimportant in a society that supposedly places its greatest value on telecommunication and interpersonal skills. Indeed, during the past two decades many career advisors have emphasized networking as the key to getting a job; writing résumés and letters are considered relatively unimportant job search skills. Some even advise job seekers to dispense with the résumé altogether and, instead, rely on cold-calling telephone techniques and "showing up" networking strategies.

But such advice is misplaced and misses one of the most important points in the job search. Résumés are an **accepted** means of communicating qualifications to employers; they are becoming essential requirements for today's new electronic recruitment operations. Employers expect to receive well-crafted résumés that represent the best professional efforts of candidates. The problem is that hiring officials receive so many poorly written and distributed résumés. Indeed, many candidates might be better off not writing a résumé given the weaknesses they demonstrate by producing poorly constructed résumés. Failure to develop a well-crafted résumé will disqualify you for many jobs.

Résumés do not substitute for other equally important communication activities, but they do play a critical transformational role in your job search. They must be carefully linked to other key job search activities, especially networking and informational interviews which function as important **methods for disseminating résumés**.

You simply must write a résumé if you are to be taken seriously in today's job market. And you will be taken most seriously if you write and disseminate dynamite résumés.

While some individuals do get interviews without writing résumés, you can do much better if you take the time and effort to develop a well-crafted résumé and disseminate it properly. It should be designed for both electronic and human consumption. Your résumé should focus on the employer's needs. It should demonstrate your professionalism, competence, and personality. Without an effective résumé, your job search will have a limited impact on potential employers.

Improve Your Effectiveness

Just how effective are you in opening the doors of potential employers? In addition to writing a dynamite résumé, what other things should you be doing to improve the effectiveness of job search?

Let's begin by identifying your level of job search information, skills, and strategies as well as those you need to develop and improve. You can do this by completing the "job search competencies" exercise on pages 11-12.

INSTRUCTIONS: Respond to each statement by circling the number on the right that best represents your situation.

SCALE:

1 = strongly agree	4 = disagree
2 = agree	5 = strongly disagree
3 = maybe, not certain	

1. I know what motivates me to excel at work.   1 2 3 4 5

2. I can identify my strongest abilities and skills.   1 2 3 4 5

3. I can identify at least seven major achievements that clarify a pattern of interests and abilities that are relevant to my job and career.   1 2 3 4 5

4. I know what I both like and dislike in work.   1 2 3 4 5

5. I know what I want to do during the next 10 years.   1 2 3 4 5

6. I have a well-defined career objective that focuses my job search on particular organizations and employers.   1 2 3 4 5

7. I know what skills I can offer employers in different occupations.   1 2 3 4 5

8. I know what skills employers most seek in candidates.   1 2 3 4 5

9. I can clearly explain to employers what I do well and enjoy doing.   1 2 3 4 5

10. I can specify why employers should hire me.   1 2 3 4 5

11. I can gain support of family and friends for making a job or career change.   1 2 3 4 5

12. I can find 10 to 20 hours a week to conduct a part-time job search.   1 2 3 4 5

13. I have the financial ability to sustain a three-month job search.   1 2 3 4 5

14. I can conduct library and interview research on different occupations, employers, organizations, and communities.   1 2 3 4 5

15. I can write different types of effective résumés
and job search/thank-you letters.   1   2   3   4   5

16. I can produce and distribute résumés and letters
to the right people.   1   2   3   4   5

17. I can list my major accomplishments in action terms.   1   2   3   4   5

18. I can identify and target employers with whom
I want to interview.   1   2   3   4   5

19. I can develop a job referral network.   1   2   3   4   5

20. I can persuade others to join in forming a job
search support group.   1   2   3   4   5

21. I can prospect for job leads.   1   2   3   4   5

22. I can use the telephone to develop prospects
and get referrals and interviews.   1   2   3   4   5

23. I can plan and implement an effective direct-mail
job search campaign.   1   2   3   4   5

24. I can generate one job interview for every 10 job
search contacts I make.   1   2   3   4   5

25. I can follow-up on job interviews.   1   2   3   4   5

26. I can negotiate a salary 10-20% above what an
employer initially offers.   1   2   3   4   5

27. I can persuade an employer to renegotiate my salary
after six months on the job.   1   2   3   4   5

28. I can create a position for myself in an organization.   1   2   3   4   5

TOTAL   _____

You can calculate your overall job search effectiveness by adding the numbers
you circled for a composite score. If your total score is more than 75 points, you
need to work on developing your job search skills. How you scored each item
will indicate to what degree you need to work on improving specific job search

skills. If your score is under 50 points, you are well on your way toward job search success. In either case, this book should help you better focus your job search around the critical writing skills necessary for communicating your qualifications to employers. Other books can assist you with many other important aspects of your job search.

Get Taken Seriously By Employers

The whole purpose of a job search is to get taken seriously by strangers who have the power to hire you. Your goal is to both discover and land a job you really want. You do this by locating potential employers and then persuading them to talk to you by telephone and in person about your interests and qualifications.

Being a stranger to most employers, you initially communicate your interests and qualifications on paper in the form of résumés and cover letters. How well you construct these documents will largely determine whether or not you will proceed to the next stage—the job interview.

The major weakness of job seekers is their inability to keep focused on their **purpose**. Engaging in a great deal of wishful thinking, they fail to organize their job search in a purposeful manner. They do silly things, ask dumb questions, and generally waste a great deal of time and money on needless activities. They frustrate themselves by going down the same deadend roads. Worst of all, they turn off employers by demonstrating poor communication skills—both written and oral.

> ❑ **The whole purpose of a job search is to be taken seriously by strangers who have the power to hire.**
>
> ❑ **The major weakness of job seekers is their inability to keep focused on their purpose.**
>
> ❑ **You should focus on improving your communication effectiveness in the job search by writing and distributing dynamite résumés.**

The average job seeker often wanders aimlessly in the job market, as if finding a job were an ancient form of alchemy. Preoccupied with job search **techniques**, they lack an overall **purpose and strategy** that would give meaning and direction to discrete job search activities. They often engage in random and time-consuming activities that have little or no payoff. Participating in a highly ego-involved activity, they quickly lose sight of what's really important to conducting a successful job search—responding to the needs of employers. Not surprisingly, they aren't taken seriously by employers because they don't take themselves and employers seriously enough to organize their activities around key qualifications that persuade employers to invite them to job interviews. This should not happen to you.

The following pages are designed to increase your power to get taken seriously by employers. Individual chapters provide a quick primer on the key principles involved in writing, producing, evaluating, distributing, and following-up your own dynamite résumé. It also presents résumé examples that illustrate the key principles involved in writing dynamite résumés.

Since the examples in this book are presented to illustrate important résumé writing **principles**, they should not be copied nor edited. As you will discover in the following pages, it is extremely important that you create your own résumés that express the "unique you" rather than send "canned" résumés to potential employers.

In the end, our goal is to improve your **communication effectiveness** in the job search. On completing this book, you should be able to write dynamite résumés that result in many more invitations to job interviews.

Do What's Expected and Produces Results

Based on experience, we assume most employers do indeed expect to receive well-crafted résumés. We proceed on the assumption that résumés are one of the most important elements in the job search. Moreover, they are becoming more important than ever given the increased use of résumé databases and electronic scanning technology for screening candidates.

The old interview adage that "you never have a second chance to make a good first impression" is equally valid for the résumé. For it is usually the résumé and cover letter rather than your telephone voice or appearance that first introduces you to a prospective employer. Your résumé tells who you are and why an employer should want to spend valuable time meeting you in person. It invites the reader to focus attention on your key qualifications in relation to the employer's needs. It enables you to set an agenda for further exploring your interests and qualifications with employers.

Once you discover the importance of writing dynamite résumés, you will never again produce other types of résumés. Your dynamite résumé will have the power to move you from stranger to interviewee to employee. It will open many more doors to job interviews and offers!

Choose the Right Resources

This book is primarily concerned with communicating your qualifications in writing to employers who, in turn, will be sufficiently motivated to invite you to a face-to-face job interview. Several of our other books deal with the key steps in the job search process as illustrated on page 8: *Change Your Job Change Your Life, Discover the Best Jobs For You, High Impact Résumés and Letters, Dynamite Cover Letters, Interview For Success, 101 Dynamite Answers to Interview Questions, Dynamite Networking For Dynamite Jobs, Dynamite Tele-Search*, and *Dynamite Salary Negotiations*. Others examine specific career fields, including government jobs, public employment strategies, the federal application form, and the special case of educators: *The Complete Guide to Public Employment, Find a Federal Job Fast, The Directory of Federal Jobs and Employers*, and *The Educator's Guide to Alternative Jobs and Careers*. If your interests include the international employment arena, we have three books that can assist you: *The Complete Guide to International Jobs and Careers, The International Jobs Directory*, and *Jobs For People Who Love Travel*. For job

> Try this Internet site for the latest information on resources for conducting a dynamite job search:
> *www.impactpublications.com*

alternatives, see our *Best Jobs For the 21st Century* and *Jobs and Careers With Nonprofit Organizations*. These and many other job search books are available from Impact Publications. For your convenience, they can be ordered by completing the form at the end of this book.

Impact Publications also publishes a brochure of additional job and career resources. To receive a free copy of this listing, send a self-addressed stamped envelope (#10 business size) to:

IMPACT PUBLICATIONS
ATTN: Career Resource List
9104-N Manassas Drive
Manassas Park, VA 20111-5211

You also may want to visit their Internet site for a complete listing of career resources: *www.impactpublications.com*. Their site contains some of the most important career and job finding resources available today, including many titles that are difficult, if not impossible, to find in bookstores and libraries. You will find everything from additional résumé books, to books on self-assessment, cover letters, interviewing, government and international jobs, military, women, minorities, students, and entrepreneurs. The catalog also includes videos, audio programs, computer software, subscriptions, and CD-ROM programs relating to jobs and careers. This is an excellent resource for keeping in touch with the major resources that can assist you with every stage of your job search.

Put Power Into Your Job Search

Whatever you do, make sure you acquire, use, and taste the fruits of job search power. You should go into the job search equipped with the necessary knowledge and skills to be most effective in communicating your qualifications to employers.

As you will quickly discover, the job market is not a place to engage in wishful thinking. It's at times impersonal, frequently ego deflating, and often unforgiving of errors. It requires clear thinking, strong organizational skills, and effective strategies for making the right moves with employers. Above all, it rewards individuals who follow-through in implementing each job search step with enthusiasm, dogged persistence, and the ability to handle rejections.

May you soon discover this power and incorporate it in your own dynamite résumé!

2

Résumé Do's and Don'ts

If you want your job search to be most effective, you must follow several principles of effective résumé writing, production, distribution, and follow-up. Equally important, you must regularly evaluate your progress and measure your performance. The principles range from obvious elementary concerns, such as correct spelling, punctuation, and placement of elements, to more complicated questions concerning when and how to best follow-up a résumé sent to an employer five days ago. Evaluation involves both internal self-evaluation mechanisms and external evaluators.

Mystery and Ritual

But before putting the principles and evaluations into practice, we need to examine the very concept of a résumé within the larger job search. What exactly are we talking about? What is this thing called a résumé and how does it relate to other steps in your job search? How do readers typically respond to résumés? What are some of the most common writing errors and mistakes one needs to avoid?

A great deal of mystery and confusion surrounds the purpose and content of résumés. Occupying a time-honored—almost ritual—place in the job finding

17

process, résumés remain the single most important document you will write and distribute throughout your job search. Do it wrong and your job search will suffer accordingly. Do it right and your résumé should open many doors that lead to job interviews and offers. The obvious choice is to write dynamite résumés for greater job search success.

Your Résumé Has Purpose

What exactly is a résumé? Is it a summary of your work history? An autobiography of your major accomplishments? A statement of your key qualifications? A catalog of your interests, skills, and experience? An introduction to your professional and personal style? Your business calling card? A jumble of keywords for triggering optical scanners?

> ❑ When reviewing your résumé, employers look for sound indicators of your *probable future performance* rather than a summary of your history.
>
> ❑ You must keep your résumé writing, production, distribution, and follow-up activities focused around your purpose—getting interviews.
>
> ❑ Résumés lacking a central focus or purpose are good candidates for mindless direct-mail approaches.
>
> ❑ Make sure your résumé is *employer-centered* rather than self-centered.

Let's be perfectly clear what we are talking about. A résumé is all of these things and much much more. It is an important **product**—produced in reference to your goals, skills, and experience—that furthers two important **processes**—"job search" for you and "screening/hiring" for employers. While it is a basic requirement when applying for many jobs, your résumé plays a central role in directing you and your job search into productive information gathering and employment channels. It communicates your goals and capabilities to potential employers who must solve personnel problems—hire someone to perform particular functions and jobs. At the very least, a résumé represents the "unique you" to others who may or may not know much about your particular mix of goals and capabilities. It may represent the potential solution to employers' problems.

Better still, let's define a résumé in terms of its **purpose** or **outcomes** for you in relation to hiring officials: *a résumé is an advertisement for an interview.* In other words, the purpose of writing, producing, distributing, and following-up a résumé is to get job interviews—nothing more, nothing less. As such, your résumé should follow certain principles of good advertising—grab attention, heighten interest, sell the product, and promote action.

Your ultimate purpose in writing a résumé is to **get employers to take ac-**

tion—conduct a telephone interview as well as invite you to the first of several job interviews which will eventually result in job offers and employment. Thus, the purpose is a specific outcome.

If you define a résumé in these terms, then the internal résumé structure and specific elements included or excluded—as well as the production, distribution, and follow-up methods you choose—become self-evident. You should only include those elements that are of interest to employers.

But what do employers want to see on your résumé? They simply want to see sound indicators of your **probable future performance** rather than a summary of your professional and personal history. They want to know if you have a high probability of **adding value** to their operations. Adding value can have several meanings depending on the employment situation—increase market shares, improve profitability, solve specific problems, become more competitive, introduce a new system for improving efficiency.

While the logic here is very simple, it nonetheless needs repeating throughout your job search. Since employers will be hiring your future, they are more concerned with your future performance—*"What can you do for me?"* —rather than "the facts" about your past—*"Where did you go to school and what did you do during the summer of 1992?"* Therefore, you must present your past in such a manner that it clearly indicates **patterns of performance** that are good predictors of your future value and performance.

Focus On Employers' Needs and Adding Value

Without this central guiding purpose in mind, your résumé is likely to take on a different form, as well as move in different directions, than outlined in this book. You simply must keep your résumé writing, production, distribution, and follow-up activities focused around your purpose—getting interviews. No distractions nor wishful thinking should interfere with this.

Your approach, whether implicit or explicit, to résumé writing says something about how you view yourself in relation to employers. It tells readers to what degree you are self-centered versus employer-centered. Are you oriented toward adding value to the employer's operations, or are you primarily concerned with acquiring more benefits for yourself? If you merely chronicle your past work history, you are likely to produce a self-centered résumé that says little or nothing about your interests, skills, and abilities in relation to the employers' needs. You say nothing about adding value to the employers' operations. Résumés lacking a central focus or purpose are good candidates for mindless direct-mail approaches—broadcasting them to hundreds of employers who by chance might be interested in your history.

On the other hand, if you thoughtfully develop a job objective that is sensitive to employers' performance needs and then relate your patterns of skills and accomplishments to that objective, you should produce a dynamite résumé. Such a resume transcends your history as it clearly communicates your qualifications to employers and suggests that you know how to add more value to the employer's operations. This type of résumé is **employer-centered**; it addresses employers' hiring needs. Such a résumé is best targeted toward a select few employers who have job opportunities appropriate for your particular mix of interests, skills, and accomplishments. Therefore, the type of résumé you produce tells employers a great deal about you both professionally and personally.

An intensely ego-involved activity, résumé writing often goes awry as writers attempt to produce a document that he or she "feels good" about. Thinking a résumé is analogous to an obituary, many writers believe their résumé should summarize what's good about them. If the central purpose is to pile on a lot of good information about the individual's past, then a résumé becomes a nonfocused dumping ground for a great deal of extraneous information employers neither need nor want. Such a résumé may include lots of interesting facts that must be left to the interpretation of the reader who, by definition, is a very busy person; few such readers have the luxury of spending time analyzing and relating someone's chronicle of work history to their specific employment needs. Your résumé may end up like most résumés—an uninspired listing of names, dates, and duties that are supposed to enlighten employers about your qualifications. While you may feel good writing such a document, don't expect employers to get excited enough to contact you for an interview. Your résumé will likely end up in their "circular files."

Every time you make a decision concerning what to include or exclude in your résumé, and how and when to produce, distribute, and follow-up your job search communications, always keep in mind your purpose: *you are advertising yourself for a job interview*. Such a single-minded purpose will serve you well. It will automatically answer many questions you may have about the details of writing, producing, distributing, and following-up your résumé. It will tell you what is and is not important in the whole résumé writing, production, distribution, and follow-up process.

Résumé Myths and Realities

Numerous myths about finding employment and contacting employers lead individuals down the wrong résumé writing paths. Keep these eleven myths and corresponding realities in mind when writing your résumé:

Myths	Realities
1. The résumé is the key to getting a job.	There is nothing magical about résumés. Indeed, there are many keys to getting a job, from being in the right place at the right time, having a good connection, to conducting an excellent job interview. The résumé is only one step, albeit an important one, in the job finding process. Other steps depend on well-crafted résumés and cover letters. Remember, your résumé is an advertisement for a job interview. Employers do not hire individuals because of the content or quality of their résumé; the résumé only gets them invited to job interviews. The job interview is the real key to getting the job; it is the prerequisite step for a job offer and employment contract. But you must first communicate your qualifications to employers through the medium of a top quality résumé in order to get the job interview.
2. The résumé is not as important to getting a job as other job search activities, such as networking and informational interviews.	Résumés still remain one of the most important written documents you will produce during your job search. If you expect to be interviewed for jobs, you simply must produce a well-crafted résumé that clearly communicates your qualifications to employers. Whether you like it or not, employers want to see you on paper **before** talking to you over the telephone or seeing you in person. And they want to see a top quality résumé—an attractive, error-free document that **represents your best self**. You should pay particular attention to the

details and exacting quality required in producing a first-rate résumé. Errors, however minor, can quickly eliminate you from consideration. Without such an error-free résumé, you seriously limit your chances of getting job interviews. And without job interviews, you won't get job offers.

3. **A résumé should primarily document your work history for employers.**

A résumé should communicate to employers how you will **add value** to their operations. You include work history on a résumé as evidence that you have a track record of adding value to other employers' operations. The assumption for the reader is that you will add similar value to his or her operations. Be sure you always describe your work history or experience in such value-added terms.

4. **It's best to send your résumé to hundreds of employers rather than to just a few.**

Power in the job search comes from selective targeting—not through numbers. It comes from making a few contacts with the right people who have a specific **need** for your particular mix of interests, skills, and qualifications. While it may be comforting to think you are making progress with your job search by sending résumés to hundreds of potential employers, in reality you create an illusion of progress that will ultimately disappoint you; few people will seriously read an unsolicited résumé and thus consider you for employment when they have no need. A résumé broadcast or "shotgun" approach to finding a job indicates a failure to seriously focus your job search around the **needs** of specific employers. Your time, effort, and money will be better spent in marketing your résumé in conjunction with other effective job search activities—networking and informational interviews. These activities force you to concentrate on specific employers who would be most interested in your interests, skills, and qualifications. These individuals have a need that will most likely coincide with both your résumé and job search timing.

5. **It's not necessary to include an objective on your résumé.**

Without an objective your résumé will lack a central focus from which to relate all other elements in your résumé. An objective gives your résumé organization and coherence. It tells potential employers that you are a **purposeful individual**—you have specific job and career goals in mind that are directly related to your past pattern of interests, skills, and experience as documented in the remainder of your résumé. If properly stated, your objective will become the most powerful and effective statement on your résumé. Without an objective, you force the employer to "interpret" your résumé. He or she must analyze the discreet elements in each résumé category and draw conclusions about your future capabilities which may or may not be valid. You force the person to engage in what may be a difficult analytical task, depending on their analytic capabilities. Therefore, it is to your advantage to control the flow and interpretation of your qualifications and capabilities by stating a clear employer-oriented objective. While you can state an objective in your cover letter, it is best to put your objective at the very beginning of your résumé. After all, letters do get detached from résumés.

On the other hand, many people prefer excluding an objective because it tends to lock them into a particular type of job; they want to be flexible. Such people demonstrate a cardinal job search sin—they really don't know what they want to do; they tend to communicate their lack of focus in their résumé as well as in other job search activities. They are more concerned with fitting into a job ("Where are the jobs?") than with finding a job fit for them ("Is this job right for me?").

6: The best type of résumé outlines employment history by job titles, responsibilities, and inclusive employment dates.

This type of résumé, the traditional chronological or "obituary" résumé, may or may not be good for you. It's filled with historical "what" information—what work you did, in what organizations, over what period of time. Such résumés tell employers little about what it is you can do for them in the future. You should choose a résumé format that clearly communicates your major strengths—not your historical background—to employers. Those strengths should be formulated as **patterns of performance** in relation to your goals and skills as well as the employer's needs. Your choice of formats include variations of the chronological, functional, and combination résumés—each offering different advantages and disadvantages, depending on your goals.

7: Employers appreciate lengthy detailed résumés because they give them more complete information for screening candidates than shorter résumés.

Employers prefer receiving short, succinct one or two-page résumés. Longer résumés lose their interest and attention. Such résumés usually lack a focus, are filled with extraneous information, need editing, and are oriented toward your past rather than the employer's future. If you know how to write a dynamite résumé, you can put all of your capabilities into a one to two-page format. These résumés only include enough information to persuade employers to contact you for an interview. Like good advertisements, they generate enough interest so the reader will contact you for more information (job interview) before investing in the product (job offer).

8. It's okay to put salary expectations and references on your résumé.

Two of the worst things you can do is to include salary information (history or expectations) and list your references on your résumé. Remember, the purpose of your résumé is to get an interview—nothing more, nothing less. Only during the interview—and preferably toward the end—should you discuss salary and share information on references.

And before you discuss salary, you want to demonstrate your **value** to hiring officials as well as learn about the **worth** of the position. Only **after** you make your impression and gather information on the job, can you realistically talk about—and negotiate—salary. You can not do this if you prematurely mention salary on your résumé. A similar principle applies to references. Never put your references on a résumé. The closest you should ever get to mentioning names, addresses, and phone numbers—other than yours—is a simple statement appearing at the end of your résumé:

"References available upon request"

You want to control your references for the interview. You should take a list of references appropriate for the position you will interview for with you to the interview. If you put references on your résumé, the employer might call someone who has no idea you are applying for a particular job. The conversation could be embarrassing. As a simple courtesy, you need to ask your references ahead of time whether you may use their name as a reference. At that point, you want to brief your reference on the position you seek, explaining why you feel you should be selected by focusing on your goals and strengths in relation to the position. Give this person information that will support your candidacy. Surprisingly, though, few employers actually follow-through by contacting stated references! This is perhaps one reason they often make poor hiring decisions. Many employers are surprised to later discover a problem employee had similar problems in previous jobs.

9: You should not include your hobbies nor any personal statements on a your résumé.

In general this is true. However, there are exceptions which would challenge this rule as a myth. If you have a hobby or a personal statement that can strengthen your objective in relation to the employer's needs, consider including it on your résumé. For example, if a job calls for someone who is outgoing and energetic, you would not want to include a hobby or personal statement that indicates that you are a very private and sedentary person, such as "enjoy reading and writing" or "collect stamps." But "enjoy organizing community fund drives" and "compete in the Boston Marathon" might be very appropriate statements for your résumé. Such statements further emphasize the "unique you" in relation to your capabilities, the requirements for the position, and the employer's needs.

10. **You should try to get as much as possible on each page of your résumé.**

Each page of your résumé should be appealing to the eye. It should make an immediate favorable impression, be inviting and easy to read, and look professional. You achieve these qualities by using a variety of layout, type style, highlighting, and emphasizing techniques. When formatting each section of your résumé, be sure to make generous use of white space. Bullet, underline, or bold items for emphasis. If you try to cram too much on each page, your résumé will look cluttered and uninviting. You may make just the opposite impression you thought you were making in an ostensibly well organized résumé—you look disorganized!

11. **Once you send a résumé to an employer, there is not much you can do except wait for a reply.**

Waiting for potential employers to contact you is not a good job search strategy. Sending a résumé to a potential employer is only the first step in connecting with a potential job. You should always **follow-up** your résumé with a phone call, preferably within seven days, to answer questions, conduct a telephone interview, get invited to a job interview, or acquire additional information, advice, and referrals. Without this follow-up action, your résumé is likely to get lost amongst many other résumés that compete for the reader's attention.

Taken together, these myths and realities emphasize one overriding concern when writing a résumé:

> The key to effective résumé writing is to give the reader, within the space of one- to two-pages, just enough interesting information about your past performance and future capabilities so he or she will get sufficiently excited to contact you for a job interview.

It is during the interview, rather than on your résumé, that you will provide detailed answers to the most important questions concerning the job. Those questions are determined by both the interviewer and you during the job interview. Don't prematurely eliminate yourself from consideration by including too much or too little information, or being too boastful or too negative, on your résumé before you get to the interview stage. In this sense, your résumé becomes an important "window of opportunity" to get invited to job interviews that hopefully will translate into good job offers.

Common Writing Errors and Mistakes

A résumé must first get written and written well. And it is at the initial writing stage that many deadly errors and mistakes get made. The most common errors occur when writers fail to keep the purpose of their résumé in mind.

Most errors kill a résumé even before it gets fully read. At best these errors leave negative impressions which are difficult to overcome at this or any other point in the hiring process. Remember, hiring officials have two major inclusion/exclusion concerns in mind when reading your résumé:

- They are looking for excuses to eliminate you from further consideration.

- They are looking for evidence to consider you for a job interview—how much value you will add to their operations.

Every time you make an error, you provide supports for eliminating you from further consideration. Concentrate, instead, on providing **supports** for being considered for a job interview.

Make sure your résumé is not "dead on arrival." To ensure against this, avoid the most common errors reported by employers who regularly review résumés:

- **Not related to the reader's interests or needs.** Not another one of these! Why was this sent to me? I don't have a job vacancy nor do we perform work related to this person's skills. Did they purchase someone's mailing list? They need to take their job search seriously by being more informed about employers and organizations before sending out such junk mail. In the meantime, this person has just wasted my time, which is both limited and precious to me. I hope they don't plan to further waste my time by following-up their résumé and letter with a phone call! I only interview and hire people when I have a vacancy—not in response to unsolicited résumés.

- **Too long, short, or condensed.** Ugh! What a waste of time and effort. Don't they have a better sense of self-esteem?

- **Poorly designed format and an unattractive appearance.** This person probably doesn't look any better than his paper presentation. I have a bad feeling about this person. I've met this type before— really boring people.

- **Misspellings, bad grammar, and wordiness.** When will they learn to write a simple sentence that conveys a basic level of literacy? This person is either illiterate or careless—two problems I don't need to hire. I wonder what other communication problems this person brings to the job? These errors are insulting. I really don't need this trouble.

- **Poor punctuation.** I wonder how much training this person will need to get up to speed? This could be an expensive hire—and fire!

- **Lengthy phrases, sentences, and paragraphs.** The language here is English. I wonder where they learned to do this? Maybe they talk the same way—on and on and on.

- **Too slick, amateurish, and "gimmicky."** I'm impressed. Yeah, I bet this person is the hottest thing since sliced bread. Just what I need—a manipulator on the payroll. I don't need gimmicks—only an enthusiastic individual who has a predictable pattern of performance.

- **Too boastful or dishonest.** I've seen this before. This one's too hot to handle—I'll regret the day I contacted him for an interview.

- **Poorly typed and reproduced.** Isn't this nice. I'm really impressed with the quality of this individual. Maybe I'm not important enough to receive a better quality résumé. Or perhaps this is their best effort!

- **Irrelevant information.** Do I really need to know height, weight, children, and spouse's name? I wonder what other irrelevances this person can bring to the interview, and the job.

- **Critical categories missing.** Where's the objective? Where did she work? Any special awards, recognitions, accomplishments? What about education? What years did this include? Don't they know what to include on a résumé?

- **Hard to understand or requires too much interpretation.** I really don't have time to do a content analysis of this individual's skills and accomplishments. After reading two pages of "bio facts," I still don't know what this person can do other than many different jobs.

> ❑ Keep your résumé short and succinct—1 to 2 pages with crisp language rich in verbs and nouns is perfect.
>
> ❑ Include all relevant categories; avoid irrelevant information that distracts from your central message.
>
> ❑ Clearly communicate a "pattern of performance" related to the employer's hiring needs.
>
> ❑ Avoid the use of "canned" resume language or anything that suggests you have not produced your own résumé.

- **Unexplained time gaps.** What did he do between 1989 and 1992? School? Unemployed? Tried to find himself Paris? A drug or criminal problem? Dropped out of life?

- **Does not convey accomplishments or a pattern of performance from which the reader can predict future performance.** Interesting, but what can the person do for me? I want to be able to predict what this person will likely do in my organization. Show me value and performance.

- **Text does not support objective.** Nicely stated objective, but there's no evidence this person has any experience or skills in line with the objective. Could this be a statement of "wishful thinking" or something that has been copied from someone else's résumé?

- **Unclear or vague objective.** What exactly does this person want to do in my organization? Does she have specific goals for the next five or ten years? Perhaps this person really doesn't know what she wants to do other than get a good paying job through me.

- **Lacks credibility and content—includes lots of fluff and "canned" résumé language.** Where do they get all this dreadful stuff? Probably using the same old résumé book that emphasizes action verbs and transferable skills but fails to advise them to include some content. Where's the beef? Show me real skills and accomplishments.

This listing of writing errors and possible reader responses emphasizes how important **both** form and content are when writing a résumé with purpose. You must select an important form, arrange each element in an attractive manner, and provide the necessary substance to grab the attention of the reader and move him or her to action. And all these elements of good résumé writing must be related to the needs of your audience. If not, you may quickly kill your résumé by committing some of these deadly errors.

Remember, hiring officials are busy people who only devote a few seconds to reading your résumé. They are seasoned at identifying errors that will effectively remove you from further consideration. They want to see you error-free on paper so they can concentrate on what they most need to do—evaluate your qualifications.

Qualities of Effective Résumés

A well-crafted résumé expresses many important professional and personal qualities employers seek in candidates:

- Your sense of **self-esteem and purpose**.

- Your **level of literacy**.

- Your **ability to conceptualize and analyze** your own interests, skills, and abilities in relation to the employer's needs.

- Your **patterns of performance and value-added behavior**.

- Your ability to clearly communicate **who you are** and **what you want to do** rather than who you have been and what you have done.

- Your **view of the employer**—how important he or she is in relation to your interests, skills, and abilities. Are you self-centered?

These qualities are expressed through certain résumé principles which you can learn and apply to most employment situations. Your résumé should

- Immediately impress the reader.

- Be visually appealing and easy-to-read.

- Indicate your career aspirations and goals.

- Focus on your value in relation to employers' needs.

- Communicate your job-related **abilities** and **patterns of performance** —not past or present job duties and responsibilities.

- Stress your productivity—potential to solve employers' problems.

- Communicate that you are a responsible and purposeful person who gets things done.

- Use a language that clearly communicates skills required by the employer—a "keyword" language that is also sensitive to résumé scanning technology.

If you keep these general principles in mind, you should be able to produce a dynamite résumé that will grab the attention of employers who will be moved to action—invite you to a job interview. To do less is to communicate the wrong messages to employers—that you may lack purpose, literacy, good judgment, and a pattern of performance.

Always Remember Your Audience and Purpose

When deciding what to include in your résumé, always remember these important writing guidelines for creating a dynamite résumé:

1. View your résumé as your personal **advertisement**.

2. Focus on the purpose of your résumé which is to get a **job interview**.

3. Take the offensive by developing a résumé that **structures the reader's thinking** around your objective, qualifications, strengths, and projections of future performance.

4. Make your résumé **generate positive thinking** rather than raise negative questions or confuse readers.

5. Focus your résumé on the **needs of your audience**.

6. Communicate clearly what it is you **want to do and can do** for the reader.

7. Always be **honest** without being stupid. Stress your positives; never volunteer nor confess your negatives.

If you keep these basic purposes and principles in mind, you should produce a dynamite résumé as well as conduct a job search that is both purposeful and positive. Your résumé should stand out above the crowd as you clearly communicate your qualifications to employers.

In the next two chapters we'll take an in-depth look at these and several other principles relevant to the whole spectrum of résumé activities—writing, producing, distributing, following-up, and evaluating.

3

66 Writing, Production, Distribution, & Follow-Up Principles

Effective résumés follow certain writing, production, distribution, and follow-up principles that are specific to the résumé medium and relevant to the job search. These principles should be incorporated into every stage of the résumé writing, production, distribution, and follow-up process. If you fail to incorporate these résumé principles, your job search will most likely fail to reach its full potential.

Writing

Overall Strategy

1. **Do first things first by making sure your résumé represents the "unique you":** Avoid creatively plagiarizing others' résumés, however tempting and easy to do. A widely abused approach to résumé writing, creative plagiarizing occurs when someone decides to take shortcuts by writing their résumé in reference to so-called "outstanding résumé examples"; they basically edit the examples by substituting

information on themselves for what appears in the example. The result is a résumé filled with a great deal of "canned" résumé language that may be unrelated to the individual's goals, skills, and experience.

The best résumés are those based on a thorough self-assessment of your interests, skills, and abilities which, in turn, is the **foundation** for stating a powerful objective, shaping information in each category, and selecting proper résumé language. What, for example, do you want to do before you die? Answering this question in detail will tell you a great deal about your values and goals in relation to your career objectives. You may want to incorporate this information into your résumé. Do first things first by starting with a self-assessment that will help you build each section of your résumé. Numerous exercises and instruments are available for conducting your own self-directed assessment of your interests, skills, and abilities.

> Avoid creatively plagiarizing others' résumés, however tempting and easy to do. Such a résumé will not accurately reflect your qualifications.

These are outlined in several other career planning and job search books we and others have written. Several are identified in the "Career Resources" section at the very end of this book. Professional testing centers and career counselors also administer a variety of useful self-assessment devices. Information on such services is readily available through your local community college, adult education programs, or employment services office.

2. **Develop a plan of action relevant to your overall job search:** Make sure your résumé reflects your career goals and is part of your larger job search plan. In addition to incorporating self-assessment data, it should be developed with specific goals in mind, based on research, and related to networking and informational interviewing activities. Begin by asking yourself the broader *"What do I want to do with this résumé?"* question about the purpose of your résumé rather than narrow your focus on the traditional *"What should I include on my résumé?"* question.

Structure and Organization

3. **Select an appropriate résumé format that best communicates your goals, skills, experience, and probable future performance to employers:** Résumé format determines how you organize the information categories for communicating your qualifications to employers. It **structures the reader's thinking** about your goals, strengths, and probable future performance. If, for example, your basic organization principle is chronology (dates you worked for different employers), then you want employers to think of your qualifications in historical terms and thus deduce future performance based upon an analysis of performance **patterns** evidenced in your work history. If your basic organizational principle is skills, then you want employers to think of you in achievement terms.

   You essentially have three formats from which to choose: chronological, functional, or combination. A **chronological résumé**—often referred to as an "obituary résumé"—is the most popular résumé format but it is by no means the most appropriate. Primarily summarizing work history, this résumé lists dates and names of employers first and your duties and responsibilities second. It often includes a great deal of extraneous information. In its worst form—the traditional chronological résumé—it tells employers little or nothing about what you want to do, can do, and will do for them. In its best form—the improved chronological résumé—it communicates your purpose, past achievements, and probable future performance to employers. It includes an objective which relates to other elements in the résumé. The work experience section includes names and addresses of former employers followed by a brief description of accomplishments, skills, and responsibilities rather than formal duties and responsibilities; inclusive employment dates appear at the end. Chronological résumés should be used by individuals who have a progressive record of work experience and who wish to advance within an occupational field. One major advantage of these résumés is that they include "the beef" employers wish to see.

   Functional résumés emphasize patterns of skills and accomplishments rather than job titles, employers, and inclusive employment dates. These résumés should be used by individuals making a significant career change, first entering the work force, or re-entering the job market after a lengthy absence. Since many employers still look for names, dates, and direct work experience—the so-called "beef"—this type of résumé often disappoints employers who are looking for more substantive information relating to "experience" and "qualifications." You should use a functional résumé only if your past work experience does not clearly support your objective. Otherwise, this can be a very weak resume that may raise negative questions that will disqualify you from consideration.

Combination résumés combine the best elements of chronological and functional résumés. They stress patterns of accomplishments and skills as well as include work history. Work history appears as a separate section immediately following the presentation of accomplishments and skills in an "Areas of Effectiveness" or "Experience" section. This is the perfect résumé for individuals with work experience who wish to change to a job in a related career field.

Examples of these different types of résumés are included in the remainder of this book. They are illustrated in the résumé transformations found in Chapter 5.

4. **Include all essential information categories in the proper order.** What you should or should not include in your résumé depends on your particular goals as well as your situation and the needs of your audience. When deciding on what to include or exclude on your résumé, always focus on the **needs** of the employer. What does he or she want or need to know about you? The most important information relates to your **future performance** which is normally determined by assessing your **past patterns of performance** ("experience" presented as "accomplishments," "outcomes," "benefits," or "performance"). At the very least your résumé should include the following five categories of information which help provide answers to five major questions:

Information category	Relevant question
Contact information	Who you are/how to contact you.
Objective	What you **want to do**.
Experience	What you **can do**—your patterns of skills and accomplishments.

Work history	What you **have done**.
Educational background	What you **have learned** and what you might be capable of learning in the future.

Taken together, these information categories and questions provide evidence for answering a sixth unanswered question:

What you will most likely do in the future.

Finding answers to this implicit question is the employer's ultimate goal in the hiring process. Employers must deduce the answer from examining what you said in each category of your one- to two-page résumé. Employers must make an important **judgment** about your future performance **with them** by carefully considering what you want to do (your objective), what you can do (your experience), and what you have done and learned (your work history and education). A résumé incorporating only these five categories of information should be sufficiently powerful to answer most employers' critical questions.

Other information categories often found on résumés include:

- Military experience
- Community involvement
- Professional affiliations
- Special skills
- Interests and activities
- Personal statement

5. **Sequence the categories according to the principle "What's most important to both you and the employer should always appear first":** You want your most important information and your strongest qualifications to always come first. Recent graduates with little or no relevant work experience, for example, should put education first since it's probably their most important "qualification" at this stage of their worklife. Your educational experience tells employers what you may have learned and thus provides some evidence of a certain knowledge, skill, and motivational base from which you possess a **capacity** to

learn and grow within the employer's organization, i.e., you are functionally trainable. Your education also may include important work experience and achievements that indicate a pattern of future performance. Education should also come first in cases where education is an important **qualifying criterion**, especially for individuals with professional degrees and certifications: teachers, professors, doctors, nurses, lawyers, accountants, counselors. Recent graduates with little or no work experience may also want to put education first. The sequence of elements should be:

- Contact information
- Education
- Experience
- Work history

Students or others with little or no work history should omit the "Work history" category (putting little or no information here can be a negative) but convert "Experience" into a new and expanded category: "Areas of Effectiveness" or "Capabilities." This section becomes the central focus that defines a functional résumé.

If you have a few or several years of direct work experience that supports your objective, and if education is not an important qualifying criteria, then your "Experience" section should immediately follow your objective. In this case "Education" moves toward the end of the résumé:

- Contact information
- Experience
- Work history
- Education

Any other categories of information should appear either immediately after "Work history" or after "Education."

6. **Avoid including extraneous information which is unrelated to your objective or to the needs of employers:** However ego-involved you become in the résumé writing process, always remember your goal and your audience. You are writing to a potential employer who

by definition is a critical stranger who has specific needs and problems he hopes to solve through the hiring process. You are not writing to your mother, spouse, lover, friends, or former teachers. The following extraneous information often appears on résumés:

- **The word "Résumé" at the top:** The reader already knows this is your résumé, assuming you have chosen a standard résumé format. It's not necessary to label it as such.

- **Present date:** This goes on your cover letter rather than your résumé.

- **Picture:** Include a picture only if it is essential for a job, such as in modeling or theater. A picture may indeed be worth "a thousand words," but 990 of those words you don't need distracting from the central focus of your résumé! Regardless of what you and your family may think about your picture—even those wonderful glamour shots—it's safe to assume that 50 percent of your readers will like and another 50 percent will dislike your picture. You don't need this type of distraction. Concentrate instead on the words and information **you** can control.

- **Race, religion, or political affiliation:** Include this information only if these are bonafide occupational qualifications, which they should not be given current anti-discrimination and equal opportunity laws.

- **Salary history or requirements:** Never ever include salary history or expectations on your résumé. If you are forced to submit this information at the initial screening stage, do so in your cover letter. Salary usually is negotiable. The salary question should only arise at the end of the interview or during the job offer—after you have had a chance to assess the worth of the job as well as demonstrate your value to hiring officials. When you include salary information on your résumé, you prematurely give information on your value before you have a chance to demonstrate your value in job interviews.

- **References:** Always make your references "available upon request." You want to control the selection of references as well as alert your references that you are applying for a specific position and that they may be contacted.

- **Personal information such as height, weight, age, sex, marital status, health:** Few, if any, of these characteristics strengthen or relate to your objective. Many are negatives. Some could be positives, but only if you are a model, karate instructor, or applying for a position which views these as bonafide occupational qualifications.

- **Any negative information:** Employment gaps, medical or mental problems, criminal records, divorces, terminations, conflicting interests. There is absolutely no reason for you to volunteer potential negatives on your résumé. This is the quickest way to get eliminated from consideration. Always remember that your résumé should represent your very "best self." If hiring officials are interested in learning about your negatives, they will ask you and you should be prepared to respond in a positive manner—but only at the interview stage.

Since most of this extraneous information is a real negative in the eyes of employers—and has little to do with your supporting your objective as well as answering employers' six critical questions—avoid including this information on your résumé.

Contact Information

7. **Put all essential contact information at the very top of your résumé as the header:** The very first element a reader should encounter on your résumé is an attractive header. At the very minimum, this header should include your name, address, and phone, fax, or e-mail numbers displayed in one of several alternative layouts:

JAMES LAWSON
8891 S. Hayward Blvd.
Buffalo, NY 14444
Tel. 707/321-9721
LawsonJ.@aol.com

JAMES LAWSON   LawsonJ.@aol.com

8891 S. Hayward Blvd.   Buffalo, NY 14444   Tel. 707/321-9721

JAMES LAWSON

8891 S. Hayward Blvd.   Tel. 707/321-9721
Buffalo, NY 14444   LawsonJ.@aol.com

JAMES LAWSON
LawsonJ.@aol.com

8891 S. Hayward Blvd.   Buffalo, NY 14444   Tel. 707/321-9721

JAMES LAWSON
8891 S. Hayward Blvd.
Buffalo, NY 14444   Tel. 707/321-9721   LawsonJ.@aol.com

We prefer capitalizing the name, although using upper and lower case letters is fine. We also prefer the first header because it introduces a very neat, clean, and eye-pleasing résumé layout which is very inviting to readers who quickly survey résumés. We use this format extensively in the examples throughout this book.

8. **Include your complete contact information:** Employers want to know how to contact you immediately should they have any questions or wish to invite you to an interview. Therefore, include

only information which enables the employer to make such a quick contact. Be sure to include **complete** contact information—name, address, phone and fax number, and e-mail address. Avoid using P.O. Box numbers; they communicate the wrong message about your housing situation—you do not have a stable address. Also, include a daytime telephone number through which you can be reached. If you do not have a telephone, or if your only daytime number is with your present employer, enlist a telephone answering service or use someone else's number who will be available and willing to screen your calls. They, in turn, can contact you at work and then you can return the call. Include your first and last name, and maybe your middle initial, depending on your professional style. The use of a middle initial is the sign of greater formality and is most frequently used by established professionals. However, using your full first, middle, and last name together is too formal: ROBERT DAVID ALLAN. If you prefer using your middle name rather than first name, do so either alone or in combination with your first initial: ROBERT ALLAN or J. ROBERT ALLAN. Do not include nick names (ROBERT "BUDZY" ALLAN) unless you feel it will somehow help your candidacy, which it most likely will not! Include any professional titles, such as M.D., Ph.D., J.D., immediately after your last name: ROBERT ALLAN, J.D. Never begin your name with a formal gender designation: Mr., Mrs., or Ms. Your address should be complete, including a zip code number. It's okay to abbreviate the state (NY for New York, IL for Illinois, CA for California) as well as certain common locational designations: N. for North, SW for Southwest, Ave. for Avenue, St. for Street, Blvd. for Boulevard, Apt. for Apartment. However, it's best to spell out Circle, Terrace, or Lane. Be sure to include your telephone number; you may want to preface it with "Tel." or "Tel:". If you have a fax number and/or e-mail address, you may want to include them immediately following your phone number:

    Tel. 819/666-2197
    Fax 819/666-2222
    AllanB@aol.com

If you are applying for a position abroad, be sure to include a fax number and/or e-mail address. Do not clutter your header with extraneous information, such as age, marital status, sex, height, and weight. Such information is totally irrelevant—indeed a negative— on a résumé. It communicates the wrong messages and indicates you don't know how to properly present yourself to potential employers. These are not qualifying criteria for most jobs. Such information should never be volunteered during your job search. Moreover, most is illegal information for employers to elicit from candidates.

Objective

9. **Include a job or career objective relevant to your skills, employers' needs, and the remaining elements of your résumé:** While some résumé advisors consider an objective to be an optional item— preferring to keep it general or place it in a cover letter—or provide little guidance on how to structure an objective and relate it to other résumé elements, we strongly recommend including a powerful objective at the very beginning of your résumé. Otherwise you neglect the critical issue of **focus**. Your objective should be the **central organizing element** from which all other elements in your résumé flow. It should tell employers what it is you **want to do**, **can do**, and **will do** for them.

   Put in its most powerful form, your objective should be employer-centered rather than self-centered. It should incorporate both a skill and an outcome in reference to your major strengths and employer's major needs. Rather than being a statement of wishful thinking ("A position in management") or opportunistic ("A research position with opportunity for career advancement"), it should focus on your major strengths **in relation to** an employer's needs. Take, for example, the following objective statement:

   > A position in data analysis where skills in mathematics, computer programming, and deductive reasoning will contribute to new systems development.

   This type of objective follows a basic **job—skill—benefit** format:

I want a _____ where I will use my
            position/job
_____ which will result in _____
    skills and abilities   outcomes and benefits.

Restated in this basic format, the above objective would appear in this form:

A data analysis job where I will use my skills in mathematics, computer programming, and deductive reasoning which will result in new systems development.

An objective based on this originating statement follows a very specific form. The first part of this objective statement emphasizes a specific position in relation to your strongest skills or abilities; the second part relates your skills to the employer's needs. Such an objective becomes a statement of **benefits** employers can expect from you. All other elements in your résumé (experience, work history, education, awards) should provide **supports** for your objective. Formulated in this manner, your objective becomes the most important element on your résumé as well as in your job search; it directs all other elements appearing on your résumé, determining what should or should not be included in each section. It also gives your job search direction, focusing your efforts toward particular employers and helps you formulate well focused answers to interview questions. While formulating such an objective may be very time consuming—your two to three-line objective statement may take several days to develop and refine—the end result will be a well-focused résumé that communicates your value and benefits to employers. If you fail to include an objective on your résumé, chances are your résumé will reflect the very nature of your job search—it's probably unfocused and disorganized. You're trying to fit into jobs rather than find a job fit for you.

10. **An objective should be neither too general nor too specific:** Many résumé writers prefer developing a very general objective so their résumé can be used for many different types of jobs. However, highly generalized objectives often sound "canned" or are meaningless ("A position working with people that leads to career

advancement"); they may indicate you don't know what you really want to do. Indeed, if your purpose is to apply for many different types of jobs, you are attempting to fit into jobs rather than find jobs fit for you. You appear to lack a clear focus on what you want to do. On the other hand, a very specific objective may be too narrow for most jobs; you may appear too specialized for many positions. Another alternative is to write a separate or targeted objective, responsive to the requirements of each position, every time you send a résumé to a hiring official. This approach should result in résumés that are most responsive to the needs of individual employers. However, you may have difficulty doing this unless you have word processing capabilities that allow you to custom-design each résumé. An objective that is not too general nor too specific will serve you well for most résumé occasions. It should indicate you know exactly what you want to do without being overly specific. Look at our examples in Chapters 5 and 6 for objectives that are neither too general nor too specific.

11. **Relate all other résumé elements to your objective, emphasizing skills, outcomes, benefits, and probable future value to the employer:** All other elements appearing on your résumé should reinforce your objective. When deciding what to include or exclude on your résumé, ask yourself this question: "Will this information strengthen my objective, which emphasizes my skills in relation to the employer's needs?" If the answer is "yes," include it. If the

> **All elements in your résumé should relate to, as well as support, your objective.**

answer is "no," exclude it. Remember, the most effective one to two-page résumé clearly and concisely communicates your objectives and strengths to employers. If you fail to organize your résumé in this manner, you are likely to include a great deal of extraneous information that communicates the wrong message to employers—you don't know what you want to do; your interests, skills, and experience are peripheral or unrelated to the reader's needs; you lack a clear focus and thus appear disorganized. These are cardinal sins committed by many résumé writers who produce self-centered résumés that fail to respond to the needs of employers. Make sure each section of your résumé clearly and consistently communicates what it is you **want to do**, **can do**, and **will do** for employers.

Summary of Qualifications

12. **You may want to include a "Summary of Qualifications" section immediately following your "Objective":** Some résumé writers prefer including a short one-line objective but immediately following it with a three or four-line "Summary of Qualifications" statement. This statement attempts to crystallize the individual's major strengths that are also relevant to the objective. It is usually a synthesis of the "Experience" section. We consider this an optional item to be used by individuals with a great deal of work experience and who choose a chronological résumé format. It is most effective on chronological résumés where the objective is weak and the experience sections are organized by position, organization, and inclusive employment dates. The "Summary of Qualifications" section enables you to synthesize in capsule form your most important skills and accomplishments as **patterns of performance**. Especially with chronological résumés, this can be a very effective section. It helps elevate your résumé by stressing major accomplishments and thus overcoming the inherent limitations of chronological résumés. An example of such a statement includes the following:

SUMMARY OF QUALIFICATIONS

Twelve years of progressively responsible experience in all phases of retail sales and marketing with major discount stores in culturally diverse metropolitan areas. Annually improved profitability by 15 percent and consistently rated in top 10 percent of workforce.

As noted in our example of Mark Able in Chapter 6, the remainer of this résumé, especially the "Experience" section, provides supports for this statement.

Work Experience

13. **Elaborate your work experience in detail with particular emphasis on your skills, abilities, and achievements:** Next to your objective, your work experience section will be the most important. Here you need to provide key details on your past skills and related accomplishments. To best develop this section, complete worksheets which include the following information on each job:

   - Name of employer
   - Address
   - Inclusive employment dates
   - Type of organization
   - Size of organization/number of employees
   - Approximate annual sales volume or annual budget
   - Position held
   - Earnings per month/year
   - Responsibilities/duties
   - Achievements or significant contributions
   - Demonstrated skills and abilities
   - Reason(s) for leaving

   We include several worksheets for generating this information in Chapter 9. It's best to complete these worksheets **before** starting to write your résumé.

14. **Keep each "Experience" section short and to the point:** Information for each job should be condensed into descriptions of five to eight lines. The language should be crisp, succinct, expressive, and direct. Keep editing—eliminate unnecessary words and phrases—until you have short, succinct, and powerful statements that grab the attention of the reader. Lengthy statements tend to lose the reader's attention and distract from your major points. The guiding principle here is to edit, edit, edit, and edit until you get it right!

15. **Work experience should be presented in the language of skills and accomplishments rather than as a listing of formal duties and responsibilities:** Employers are not interested in learning about duties and responsibilities assigned to your previous jobs which are essentially a rehash of your formal job descriptions. These come with the position regardless of who occupies the position. Instead, potential employers want to know how well you **performed** your assigned duties and responsibilities as well as any additional initiative you took that produced positive results. Since they are looking for indicators of your performance, it's to your advantage to describe your previous jobs in performance terms—what skills you used, what resulted from your work, and how your employer benefitted. These are usually termed your "accomplishments" or "achievements." An accomplishment or achievement is anything you did well that resulted in a positive outcome. Accomplishments are what define your "patterns of performance." Rather than state that your

> Responsibilities included conducting research projects assigned to office and coordinating projects with three research and development offices. Duties also involved evaluating new employees and chairing monthly review meetings.

Restate this "work experience" in terms of your actual accomplishments or achievements:

> Conducted research on transportation of hazardous wastes on interstate highways which provided the basis for new restrictive legislation (PL4921). Developed three proposals for studying the effects of toxic waste dumps on rural water supplies which received $1.75 million in funds. Chaired interdepartmental meetings that eliminated unnecessary redundancy and improved communications between technical professionals. Recommendations resulted in reorganizing R&D functions that saved the company $450,000 in annual overhead costs.

Accomplishment statements set you apart from so many other résumés that primarily restate formal duties and responsibilities assigned to positions as "Experience." Keep focused on employers' needs by stressing your accomplishments in each of your experience statements and descriptions.

16. **Incorporate action verbs and use the active voice when describing your experience:** Some of the most powerful language you can use in a résumé incorporates action or transitive verbs. It emphasizes taking action or initiative that goes beyond just formal assigned duties and responsibilities. If your grammar rules are a bit rusty, here are some examples of action or transitive verbs:

administered	conducted
analyzed	coordinated
assisted	created
communicated	designed
developed	planned
directed	proposed
established	recommended
evaluated	recruited
expanded	reduced
generated	reorganized
implemented	revised
increased	selected
initiated	streamlined
investigated	supervised
managed	trained
negotiated	trimmed
organized	wrote

When applied to the active voice, action or transitive verbs follow a particular grammatical pattern:

Subject	Transitive Verb	Direct Objective
I	increased	profits
I	initiated	studies
I	expanded	production

If written in the passive voice, these examples would appear in the "Experience" section of a résumé in the following form—which you should avoid:

"Profits were increased by 32 percent."

"The studies resulted in new legislation."

"Production was expanded by 24 percent."

The passive voice implies the object was subjected to some type of action but the source of the action is unknown. If written in the active voice, these same examples would read as follows:

"Increased profits by 32 percent."

"Initiated studies that resulted in new legislation."

"Expanded production by 24 percent."

When using action verbs and the active voice, the action verb implies that you, the subject, performed the action. The active voice helps elevate you to a personal performance level that gets de-emphasized, if not lost, when using the passive voice.

17. **Use "keywords" appropriate for optical scanners and resume databases:** Since more and more employers use résumé scanning software, automated applicant tracking systems, and résumé databases on the Internet to initially sort résumés based on keywords, it would be wise to incorporate as many keywords in your résumé as possible. Unlike the language of action or transitive verbs (Principle #16), keywords reflect the jargon of particular industries and employers—desired skills, interpersonal traits, duties, responsibilities, positions held, education attained, or equipment used. While many keywords are technical in nature, others can be more generic: "curriculum development," "customer service," "employee relations," "market research," "negotiations," "public speaking," "team

> **Keywords reflect the jargon of particular employers—skills, responsibilities, positions held, and equipment used.**

building." An employer may select a list of 30 keywords which will be used for searching and sorting résumés. If your résumé includes many of the words identified in the employer's keyword profile, the higher the probability your résumé will be selected for visual examination.

18. **Avoid using the personal pronoun "I":** When using the active voice, the assumption is that you are the one performing the action. As indicated in principle #16, there is no need to insert "I" when referring to your accomplishments. The use of "I" is awkward and inappropriate on a résumé. It makes your résumé too self-centered when you should be making it more employer-centered.

19. **Use numbers and percentages whenever possible to demonstrate your performance on previous jobs:** It's always best to state action and performance in some numerical fashion. Numbers command attention and communicate accomplishments. For example, take this "experience" statement:

   "Increased sales each year for five straight years."

   The same statement can be stated in more powerful numerical terms that are equally truthful:

   "Increased sales annually by 23% ($147,000) during the past five years."

   Which of these statements makes a more powerful impression on employers who are looking for evidence of performance patterns that might be transferred to their organization? To state you "increased" sales without stating by "how much" leaves a great deal to the imagination. Was it 1 percent or 100 percent? $5 or $500,000? If performance differences appear impressive, state them in numerical terms.

20. **Include quotes relevant to your performance:** Avoid including personal testimonials that are self-serving or are assumed to be solicited; they may appear dishonest to readers. But do include any special professional praise you have received from a company award

or from a performance evaluation. Statements such as "Received the Employee of the Year Award for outstanding performance" or "Praised by employer for *exceptional performance* and consistently ranked in the upper 10 percent of the workforce" can be powerful additions to your résumé.

21. **Eliminate any negative references, including reasons for leaving:** Keep your language focused on describing your accomplishments in positive terms. Never refer to your previous employers in negative terms and never volunteer information on why you left an employer, regardless of the reason. If you were terminated, volunteer this information only if asked to do so. This will usually occur during the job interview—not at the initial résumé and letter writing stage. If an employer wants this information, he or she will ask for it during a telephone or face-to-face interview.

22. **Do not include names of supervisors:** Your experience and work history sections should only include job titles, organizations, inclusive employment dates, responsibilities, and accomplishments. Names of individuals other than yourself should be subjects you address in face-to-face interviews rather than volunteer on résumés.

23. **If you choose a chronological résumé, begin with your most recent job and work backwards in reverse chronological order:** In a chronological résumé, your present or last job should always be described first. The next job should be the one before that one and so on. However, it is not necessary to include or provide detailed information on all jobs you ever held. Keep in mind that hiring officials are looking for patterns of performance. The best evidence of such patterns is found by examining your most recent employment—not what you did 10, 20, or 30 years ago. Include your most recent employment during the past 10 years. If you held several part-time or short-term jobs or your employment record goes back for many years, you can summarize these jobs under a single heading. For example

> **Part-time employment, 1995-1999.**
> Held several part-time positions—waitress, word processor,
> lab assistant—while attending college full-time.

Government employee, 1987-1994.
Served in several public works positions with both state and local government. Specialist on transportation policy in metropolitan areas with management-level experience.

24. **Be consistent in how you handle each description or summary:** The rule here is parallel construction. Each description or summary should have a similar structure and size. Use the same type of language, verb tense, grammatical structure, and punctuation in each section.

25. **For each job or skill, put the most important information first:** Since most hiring officials want to know what you can do for them, put that information first. If you choose a chronological résumé, begin with your job title and company and then stress your accomplishments. Your inclusive dates of employment should appear last, at the end of the description, rather than at the very beginning where it will tend to be the center of attention. If you choose a functional or combination résumé format, put your most important accomplishments first in relation to your objective.

26. **Be sure to account for major time gaps:** If you use a chronological résumé in which inclusive employment dates are prominent, check to see that you do not have major time gaps between jobs. You need to account for obvious time gaps. Were you in school, the military, or unemployed? If you were unemployed for a short time, you can easily handle this time gap by using years rather than exact months of a year when including dates of employment. For example, rather than state your last four jobs began and ended on one of these dates,

> June 1995 to present
>
> July 1992 to April 1995
>
> December 1990 to February 1992
>
> June 1988 to July 1990

State they began and ended on these dates:

1995 to present

1992 to 1995

1990 to 1992

1988 to 1990

If you specify exact months you began and left jobs, you encourage the reader to look for obvious time gaps and thus raise negative questions about your employment history. If you only use years, you can cover most short-term time gaps.

27. **If you are an obvious "job-hopper," you may want to choose a functional or combination résumé rather than a chronological résumé:** The job descriptions associated with a chronological résumé format will accentuate employment dates and make it easy for the reader to determine a pattern of career progression from one job to another. If you do not have a clear chronological pattern, you are well advised to choose another résumé format that accentuates your patterns of skills.

Other Experience

28. **Include "Other Experience" only if it further strengthens your objective in reference to the employer's needs or it helps account for employment time gaps:** Standard categories include:

■ **Military service:** Describe this experience as you would any other job—emphasize your skills and accomplishments. If none seem relevant to your résumé objective and employers' needs, keep this section brief by including your rank, service, assignments, and inclusive service dates. However, most military personnel have numerous skills and accomplishments they can incorporate in their résumés. Most need to do a thorough self-assessment in order to uncover their skills and accomplishments.

■ **Civic/Community/Volunteer:** You may have volunteer experience that demonstrates skills and accomplishments supporting your objective. For example, you may be involved in organizing community groups, raising funds, or operating a special youth program. These volunteer experiences demonstrate organization, leadership, and communication skills.

In each case, be sure to emphasize your accomplishments as they relate to both your objective and employers' needs.

Education and Training

29. **State complete information on your formal education, including any highlights that emphasize your special skills, abilities, and motivation:** Begin with your most recent education and provide the following details:

- Degree or diploma
- Graduation date
- Institution
- Special highlights, recognition, or achievements (optional)

The completed section might look like this:

B.A. in Sociology, 1995:
Ohio State University, Columbus, OH
Highlights:
Graduated Magna Cum Laude
Member, Phi Beta Kappa Honor Society

B.S. in Criminal Justice, 1993.
Ithaca College, Ithaca, NY
- Major: Law Enforcement Administration
- Minor: Management Information Systems
G.P.A. in concentration 3.6/4.0

If your grade point and other achievements are not exceptional, do not highlight them here. Your educational achievements may appear mediocre to the reader and thus your education will become a negative.

30. **Recent graduates with little relevant work experience should emphasize their educational background more than their work experience:** Follow the principle that one's most important qualifications should be presented first. For recent graduates with little relevant work experience, education tends to be their most important qualification for entering the world of work. In such cases the "Education" category should immediately follow the "Objective." Include any part-time jobs, work-study programs, internships, extracurricular activities, or volunteer work under "Experience" to demonstrate your motivation, initiative, and leadership in lieu of progressive work experience.

31. **It's not necessary to include all education degrees or diplomas on your résumé:** If high school is your highest level of education, include only high school. If you have a degree from both a community college and four-year college, include both under education, but eliminate reference to high school. Individuals with graduate degrees should only include undergraduate and graduate degrees.

32. **Include special training relevant to your objective and skills:** This may include specialized training courses or programs that led to certification or enhanced your knowledge, skills, and abilities. For example,

    Additional training, 1995 to present
    Completed several three-day workshops on written and oral communication skills: Making Formal Presentations, Briefing Techniques, Writing Memos, Audio-Visual Techniques.

    When including additional education and training, include enough descriptive information so the reader will know what skills you acquired. Don't be surprised if your special training is viewed as more important to an employer than your educational degrees.

Professional Affiliations

33. **Include professional affiliations relevant to your objective and skills:** While you may belong to many groups, it is not necessary to include all of them on your résumé. Select only those that appear to

support your objective and skills and would be of interest to an employer. Include the name, inclusive dates of membership, offices held, projects, certifications, or licenses. Normally the name of the group would be sufficient. However, should your involvement go beyond a normal passive dues-paying membership role, briefly elaborate on your contributions. For example,

> **American Society for Training and Development:** Served as President of Tidewater Virginia Chapter, 1993-1995. Developed first corporate training resource directory for Southeast Virginia.

Special Skills

34. **It's okay to include any special skills not covered in other sections of your résumé:** These special skills might include an ability to communicate in foreign languages, handle specific computer software programs, operate special equipment, or demonstrate artistic talent. Again, if you have special skills relevant to your objective and skills and which should appeal to employers, include them in a separate section labeled "Special Skills" or "Other Relevant Skills."

Awards and Special Recognition

35. **Include any awards or special recognition that demonstrate your skills and abilities:** Receiving recognition for special knowledge, skills, or activities communicates positive images to employers: you are respected by your peers; you are a leader; you make contributions above and beyond what is expected as "normal." However, be selective in what you include here by relating awards or special recognition received to your objective and skills. If you are seeking a computer programming position, including an award for "First Prize in Howard County's Annual Chili Cook Off" would distract from the main thrust of your résumé! But receiving the "Employee of the Year" award in your last job or "Community Achievement Award" would be impressive; both awards would get the attention of employers who would be curious to learn more about the basis for receiving such awards—a good interview question.

Interests and Activities

36. **You may want to include a personal statement on your résumé:** Normally we would not recommend including personal information on a résumé, and many résumé advisors recommend against doing so. However, there is one exception though you should include such information sparingly. In addition to keeping your résumé focused on your objective and skills as well as the employer's needs, you want to make you and your résumé appear unique in comparison to other candidates. You may be able to achieve this in a "Personal Statement" or "Special Interests" section. This section might include hobbies or avocations. For example, if you are seeking a position you know requires a high energy level and the employer looks favorably on stable, married, family-oriented employees, you might include some personal information as well as interests and activities that address these silent issues. For example, your personal data could include the following:

> **PERSONAL:** 35 . . . excellent health . . . married . . . children
> . . . enjoy challenges . . . interested in results

Alternatively, you could write a personal statement about yourself so that the reader might remember you in particular. For example,

> **SPECIAL INTERESTS:** Love the challenge of solving problems, taking initiative, and achieving results . . . be it in developing new marketing strategies, programming a computer, climbing a mountain, white water rafting, or modifying a motorcycle.

Such statements can give hobbies and special talents and interests new meaning in reference to your objective. But again, be very careful about including such statements. More often than not, they can be a negative, distracting the reader from the most important information included on your résumé. By all means avoid trite statements that may distract from the main thrust of your résumé.

Salary History or Expectations

37. **Never include salary information on your résumé:** While hiring officials are interested in your salary history and expectations, there is no good reason for including this information on your résumé or even in your cover letter. Salary is something that needs to be negotiated, but only after you have had a chance to learn about the value of the position as well as communicate your value to the employer. This occurs at the end of the job interview and should be the very last thing you talk about or after receiving an offer of a position. If you include salary information on your résumé or in your cover letter, you are likely to prematurely eliminate yourself from consideration—your expectations are either too high or too low.

References

38. **Never include names, addresses, and phone numbers of references on your résumé:** You may want to include a final category on your résumé:

    REFERENCES: Available upon request

However, this is an empty category that does nothing to enhance your résumé. Our recommendation is to eliminate it altogether or use it to fill out a short one-page résumé. Remember, you want to control your references by providing the information upon request which usually occurs during the interview stage. If you volunteer your references on the résumé, your references may be unprepared to talk about you to employers. It's best to list the names, addresses, and phone numbers of your professional references on a separate sheet of paper, but take that list with you to the job interview rather than volunteer the information on your résumé. Ask your references for permission to use their names and brief them on your interests in relation to the position. Make sure they have a copy of your résumé for reference.

Other Information

39. **You may want to include a few other categories of information on your résumé, depending on your experience and the relevance of such information to employers:** Consider including the following categories on your resumes:

   - Certificates
   - Accreditations
   - Licenses
   - Publications
   - Patents
   - Foreign languages
   - Government clearances

   However, include them only if they strengthen your qualifications in reference to the needs of hiring officials. For example, if foreign languages are important to employers, include them on your résumé. If you are in a professional field that requires certificates and licenses, include the appropriate information on your résumé.

Language, Style, and Tone

40. **Use an appropriate language to express your productivity and your understanding of the employer's needs:** In addition to using action verbs and the active voice, try to use the language of the employer when describing your skills and experience. Use the "jargon" of the industry in demonstrating your understanding of the employer. Be especially sensitive to "keywords" that best represent the skills and experience desired by employers. As previously noted (Principle #17), this type of language will serve you well if your résumé is electronically scanned using résumé scanning software and automated applicant tracking systems or accessed from a résumé database. Always stress your value in relation to the employer's needs—you will **add value** to the employer's operations!

41. **Use crisp, succinct, expressive, and direct language:** Avoid poetic, bureaucratic, vernacular, and academic terms that often tend to turn off readers. For example, instead of stating your objective as:

    > I would like to work with a consulting firm where I can develop new programs and utilize my decision-making and system-engineering experience. I hope to improve your organization's business profits.

    Re-word the objective so it reads like this:

    > An increasingly responsible research and development position, where proven decision-making and system engineering abilities will be used for improving productivity.

    Use the first person, but do not refer to yourself as "I" or "the author." The use of action verbs and the active voice implies you are the subject. Always use active verbs and parallel sentence structure. Avoid introductory and wind-up phrases like "My duties included . . ." or "Position description reads as follows . . ." Do not use jargon unless it is appropriate to the situation or enhances your keywords.

42. **Select an appropriate résumé language that is particularly sensitive to today's résumé scanning technology:** You should pay particular attention to the specific language you select for your résumé. Indeed, the language component of résumés is now more important than ever in the history of résumé writing. Given recent changes in employer résumé screening techniques, there's a high probability your résumé will be electronically scanned sometime during your job search. The key to getting your résumé "read" in electronic screening systems is the specific language you incorporate in your résumé. When scanning résumés electronically, employers select certain **keywords** which should appear on your résumé. If you want to increase your probability of being "electronically acceptable" to employers, you must incorporate such keywords in your résumé writing. For more information on the language requirements for electronically scanned résumés, see Peter D. Weddle, *Internet Résumés* (Manassas Park, VA: Impact Publications, 1995); Joyce Lain Kennedy and Thomas J. Morrow, *Electronic Résumé Revolution* (New York: Wiley & Sons, 1996); Pat Criscito, *Résumés in*

Cyberspace (Hauppauge, NY: Barrons, 1997); and James C. Gonyea, *Electronic Résumés* (New York: McGraw-Hill, 1996).

Appearance and Visual Techniques

43. **Use appropriate highlighting and emphasizing techniques:** The most important information on a one or two-page résumé needs to be highlighted since many readers will only spend a few seconds skimming your résumé. The most widely used highlighting and emphasizing techniques involve CAPITALIZING, underlining, *italicizing*, and **bolding** headings, words, and phrases or using bullets (●), boxes (■), hyphens (—), or asterisks (*). However, use these techniques sparingly. Overuse of highlighting and emphasizing techniques can distract from your message. A major exception to this general rule relates to electronic résumés: avoid using italics, script, and underlining if your résumé is likely to be electronically scanned.

44. **Follow the "less is more" rule when deciding on format and type style:** The fear of not getting all information onto one page leads some résumé writers to create crowded and cramped résumés that are most uninviting to read. Be sure to leave ample margins—at least 1" top to bottom and left to right—and white space. Use a standard type style (Times Roman but not Helvetica) and size (10-11 point). Remember, the first thing a reader sees is layout, white space, and type style and size. Your résumé should first be pleasing to the eye.

45. **Do not include special borders, graphics, or photos unless you are applying for a job in graphic arts or a related field:** Keep the design very basic and conservative. Special graphics effects are likely to distract from your central message. However, if you are in the graphics art or related art field, you may want to dress up your résumé with graphics that demonstrate your creativity and style. Your photo does not belong on a résumé. The rule of thumb for photos is this: Regardless of how great you or your mother may think you look in the photo, at least 50 percent of résumé recipients will probably dislike your photo—and you. The photo gives them something to pick apart—your hairstyle, smile, eyes, color, dress. Why set yourself up by including a photo that will probably work

against you? Your ego is best served with an invitation to an interview based solely on the content of your résumé. Focus on your language rather than your photo.

Résumé Length

46. **Keep sentences and sections short and succinct:** Keep in mind your readers will spend little time reading your résumé. The shorter and more succinct you can write each section and sentence, the more powerful will be your message. Try to limit the length of each job description paragraph to five to eight lines—no more than ten.

47. **Limit your résumé to one or two pages:** We agree with most résumé advisors that the one- to two-page résumé is the most appropriate, although one-page is preferable. We prefer it because it focuses the busy reader's attention on a single field of vision. It's especially reader-friendly if designed with the use of highlighting and emphasizing techniques. The one-page résumé is a definite asset considering the fact that many hiring officials must review hundreds of résumés each week. Research clearly demonstrates that retention rates decrease as one's eyes move down the page and nearly vanish on a second or third page! At first the thought of writing a one or two-page résumé may pose problems for you, especially if you think your résumé should be a presentation of your life history. However, many executives with 25-years of experience, who make $100,000 or more a year, manage to get all their major qualifications onto a one-page résumé. If they can do it, so can you. When condensing information on yourself into a one-page format, keep in mind that your résumé is an advertisement for a job interview. You only want to include enough information to grab the attention of the reader who hopefully will contact you for a job interview. If you must present your qualifications in two pages rather than one, consider making the second page a "continuation page" that provides additional details on the qualifications outlined on the first page. Two résumé examples using the continuation page are presented in Chapters 5 (James C. Astor) and 6 (Michele R. Folger).

Production

Employers also want to see your best professional effort at the production stage of résumé writing. This involves making the right choices on paper color, weight, and texture as well as production methods. Above all, the résumé they receive must be error free or they are likely to discard it as an example of incompetence.

48. **Carefully proofread and produce two or three drafts of your résumé before producing the final copies:** Be sure to carefully proofread the résumé for grammatical, spelling, and punctuation errors before producing the final camera-ready copy. Assuming you are word processing your résumé, be sure to run the spell-check and grammatik programs. Any spelling, grammatical, or punctuation errors will quickly disqualify you with employers. Read and reread the draft several times to see if you can improve various elements to make it more readable and eye appealing. Read for both form and content. Have someone else also review your résumé and give you feedback on its form and content. Use the evaluation forms in Chapter 4 to conduct both internal and external evaluations.

49. **Choose white, off-white, ivory, or light grey 20 to 50 lb. bond paper with 100% cotton fiber ("rag content"):** Your choice of paper—color, weight, and texture—do make a difference to résumé readers. These things say something about your professional style. Choose a poor quality paper and inappropriate color and you communicate the wrong messages to employers. There is nothing magical about ivory or off-white paper. As more and more people use these colors, off-white and ivory colors have probably lost their effectiveness. To be different, try a light grey or basic white. Indeed, white paper gives a nice bright look to what has become essentially a dull colored process. Stay with black ink or use a dark navy ink for the light grey paper. If you are applying for a creative position, you may decide to use more daring colors to better express your creative style and personality. However, stay away form dark colored papers. Résumés should have a light bright look to them. The paper should also match your cover letter and envelope.

50. **Produce your résumé on 8½ x 11" paper:** This is the standard business size that you should follow. Other sizes are too unconventional and thus communicate the wrong message to readers.

51. **Print only on one side of the paper:** Do not produce a two-sided résumé. If your résumé runs two pages, print it on two separate pages.

52. **Use a good quality machine and an appropriate typeface:** It's best to produce your camera-ready copy (for reproduction) on a letter quality printer, preferably a laser printer, or have it typeset. Avoid manual typewriters that produce uneven type and look very amateurish. Never produce your résumé on a dot matrix printer. Most such printers produce poor quality type that communicates a "mass production" quality. If you use a desktop publishing program, choose serif typefaces (Times Roman, Palatino, New Century). Avoid sans serif typefaces (Gothic, Helvetica, Avant Garde) which are difficult to read. Be sure you print dark crisp type.

    Most individuals reproduce their résumé on a copy machine. Indeed, given the high quality reproduction achieved on many copy machines available at local print shops, it's not necessary to go to the expense of having your résumé professionally printed. However, if you need 2000 or more copies—which is most unlikely unless you resort to a broadcast or "shot-gun" marketing approach—it may be more cost effective to have them printed. Just take your camera-ready copy, along with your choice of paper, to a local printer and have them make as many copies as you need. The cost per copy will run anywhere from 3¢ to 15¢, depending on the number of copies run. The larger the run, the cheaper will be your per unit cost.

Marketing and Distribution

Your résumé is only as good as your marketing and distribution efforts. What, for example, will you do with your résumé once you've completed it? How can you best get it into the hands of individuals who can make a difference in your job search? Are you planning to send it in response to vacancy announcements and want ads? Maybe you plan to broadcast it to hundreds of employers in the hope someone will call you for an interview? Should you include your résumé in the resume databases of various Internet employment sites? Perhaps you only want to send it to a few people who can help you with your job search? Or maybe you really don't have a plan beyond getting it produced in a "correct" form.

53. **It's best to target your résumé on specific employers rather than broadcast it to hundreds of names and addresses:** Broadcasting or "shotgunning" your résumé to hundreds of potential employers will give you a false sense of making progress with your job search since you think you are actually making contact with numerous employers. However, you will be disappointed with the results. For every 100 résumés you mail, you will be lucky to get one positive response which leads to a job interview. Indeed, many individuals report no responses after mass mailing hundreds of résumés. It's always best to **target** your résumé on specific employers through one or two methods:

■ **Respond to vacancy announcements or want ads:** Résumés sent in response to job listings also will give you a sense of making progress with your job search. Since competition is likely to be high for advertised positions, your chances of getting a job interview may not be good, although much better than if you broadcasted your résumé to hundreds of employers who may not have openings.

■ **Target employers with information on your qualifications:** The most effective way of getting job interviews is to network for information, advice, and referrals. You do this by contacting friends, professional associates, acquaintances, and others who might have information on jobs related to your interests and skills. You, in effect, attempt to uncover job vacancies before they become publicized or meet an employment need not yet recognized by employers who may create a position for you in line with your qualifications. The résumé plays an important role in this networking process. In some cases, you will be referred to someone who is interested in seeing your résumé; when that happens, send it along with a cover letter and follow-up your mailing with a telephone call. In other cases, you will conduct informational interviews with individuals who can give you advice and referrals relevant to your career interests. You should take your résumé to the informational interview and at the very end of your meeting ask your informant to critique your résumé. In the process of examining your résumé, your informant is likely to give you good feedback for further revising your résumé as well as refer you and your résumé to others. If you regularly repeat this networking and informational interviewing process, within a few weeks you should begin landing job interviews directly related to the qualifications you outlined in your dynamite résumé!

54. **The best way to broadcast your résumé is to enter it into résumé databases or use bulletin boards on the Internet:** We view the résumé databases operated by various Internet employment sites as a new form of high-tech résumé broadcasting. Résumés in these databases, which can be from 500 to 50,000 in number, are usually accessed by employers who search for candidates who have a particular mix of "keywords" on their résumé. If you have the right combination of skills and experience and know how to write a dynamite résumé with language sensitive to the search and retrieval software, you should be able to connect with employers through such electronic mediums.

55. **Learn to properly send your résumé by e-mail.** More and more employers request that résumés be sent to them by e-mail rather than by regular mail or by fax. The principles for producing and distributing (formatting, type style, etiquette, etc.) an e-mailed résumé differ from those relevant for a paper résumé sent by mail or faxed. If you communicate a great deal with employers on the Internet, you will need to frequently transmit an e-mail version of your resume. Make sure you know how to write and distribute a first-class e-mailed resume.

56. **Your résumé should always be accompanied by a cover letter:** A résumé unaccompanied by a cover letter is a naked résumé—like going to a job interview barefooted. The cover letter is very important in relation to the résumé. After all, if sent through the

mail, the letter is the first thing a hiring official reads before getting to the résumé. If the letter is interesting enough, the person proceeds to read the résumé. A well-crafted cover letter should complement rather than repeat the content of your résumé. It should grab the reader's attention, communicate your purpose, and convince the reader to take action. See our *Dynamite Cover Letters* and *201 Dynamite Job Search Letters* books for an extended discussion of the principles of effective cover letter writing, production, distribution, and follow-up. If you neglect the cover letter, you may effectively kill your résumé! In many cases, your cover letter may be more important than your résumé in landing an interview and getting the job. Your cover letter should command as much attention as your résumé.

57. **Never enclose letters of recommendation, transcripts, or other information with your résumé unless requested to do so:** Unsolicited letters of recommendation are negatives. Readers know they have been specially produced to impress them and thus they may question your integrity. Like personal photos, unsolicited transcripts may communicate negative messages, unless you have perfect grades. Such information merely distracts from your résumé and cover letter. It does not contribute to getting a job interview. It indicates you do not know what you are doing by including such information with your résumé and letter.

58. **Your résumé should be addressed to a specific person:** Always try to get the correct name and position of the person who should receive your résumé. Unless you are specifically instructed to do so, addressing your correspondence to "Dear Sir," "Director of Personnel," or "To Whom It May Concern" is likely to result in lost correspondence; the mail room may treat it as junk mail. If you later follow-up your correspondence with a phone call, you have no one to communicate with. A couple of phone calls should quickly result in the proper name. Just call the switchboard or a receptionist and ask the following:

> "I need to send some correspondence to the person in charge of _____. Whom might that be? And what is the correct address?"

Keep in mind that the people who have the power to hire are usually not in the Personnel Office; they tend to be the heads of operating units. So target your résumé accordingly!

59. **Don't limit the distribution of your résumé only to vacancy announcements.** Your goal should be to get your résumé in as many hands as possible. Send it to individuals in your network—your relatives, friends, former colleagues and employers, and anyone else who might be helpful in uncovering job leads. Remember, you want to cast a big net. Let your résumé do the fishing by casting it on as many waters as possible..

60. **Enclose your résumé and letter in a matching No. 10 business envelope or in a 9 x 12" envelope:** We prefer the 9 x 12" envelope because it keeps your correspondence flat and has greater presence than the No. 10 business envelope. Keep all your stationery matching, including the 9 x 12" envelope. If, however, it's difficult to find a matching 9 x 12" envelope, go with a white or buff-colored envelope or use a U.S. Postal Service "Priority Mail" envelope.

61. **Type the envelope or mailing label rather than handwrite the address:** Handwritten addresses look too personal and amateurish, give off mixed messages, and suggest a subtle form of manipulation on your part. This is a dumb thing to do after having enclosed a professional looking résumé. Contrary to what others may tell you, in a job search handwritten addresses—and even handwritten letters or notes—do not gain more attention nor generate more positive responses; they may actually have the opposite effect—label you as being unprofessional or someone who is trying to manipulate the employer with the old handwritten technique. Typed addresses look more professional; they are consistent with the enclosed résumé. After all, this is business correspondence—not a social invitation to invite yourself to an interview. Don't confuse communicating your qualifications to employers with selling real estate, automobiles, or insurance—fields that teach salespeople to routinely "personalize" relationships with handwritten addresses and notes to potential customers. Such a sales analogy is inappropriate for your job search.

62. **Send your correspondence by first-class or priority mail or special next-day services, and use stamps:** If you want to get the recipient's immediate attention, send your correspondence in one of those colorful next-day air service envelopes provided by the U.S. Postal Service, Federal Express, UPS, or other carriers or couriers. However, first-class or priority mail will usually get your correspondence delivered within two to three days. It's best to affix a nice commemorative stamp rather than use a postage meter. A stamp helps personalize your mailing piece and does not raise questions about whose postage meter you used!

63. **Never fax or e-mail your résumé unless asked to do so by your recipient:** It is presumptuous for anyone to fax or e-mail their résumé to an employer without express permission to do so. Such faxes are treated as junk mail and e-mails are viewed as spam; they may be seen as an unwarranted invasion of private channels of communication. If asked to fax or e-mail your correspondence, be sure to follow-up by mailing a copy of the original and indicating you sent materials by fax or e-mail on a specific date as requested. The poor quality transmission of many fax machines and the bland look of most e-mail will not do justice to the overall visual quality of your résumé. You need a paper follow-up which will also remind the individual of your continuing interest in the position.

Follow-Up

Follow-up remains the least understood but most important step in any job search. Whatever you do, make sure you follow-up **all** of your job search activities. If you fail to follow-up, you are likely to get little or no response to your job search initiatives. Follow-up means taking action that gets results.

64. **Follow-up your résumé within seven days of mailing it:** Do not let too much time lapse between when you mailed your résumé and when you contact the résumé recipient. Seven days should give the recipient sufficient time to examine your communication and decide on your future status. If a decision has not been made, your follow-up action may help accelerate a decision.

65. **The best follow-up for a mailed résumé is a telephone call:** Don't expect your résumé recipient to take the initiative in calling you for an interview. State in your cover letter that you will call the recipient at a particular time to discuss your résumé:. For example,

> I will call your office on the morning of March 17 to see if
> a meeting can be scheduled at a convenient time.

And be sure you indeed follow-up with a phone call at the designated time. If you have difficulty contacting the individual, try three times to get through. After the third try, leave a message as well as write a letter as an alternative to the telephone follow-up. In this letter, inquire about the status of your résumé, mention your continued interest in the position, and thank the individual for his or her consideration.

66. **Follow-up your follow-up with a nice thank-you letter:** Regardless of the outcome of your follow-up phone call, send a nice thank-you letter based upon your conversation. You thank the letter recipient for taking the time to speak with you and to reiterate your interest in the position. While some career counselors recommend sending a handwritten thank-you note to personalize communication between you and the employer, we caution against doing so. Remember, you are engaged in a business transaction rather than in social communications. We feel a handwritten letter is inappropriate for such situations. Such a letter should be produced in a typed form and follow the principles of good business correspondence. You can be warm and friendly in what you say. The business letter form keeps you on stage—you are putting your best business foot forward.

> Avoid sending handwritten thank-you notes. Since you are attempting to develop a new business relationship, you want to demonstrate your best professional effort. Type it.

The examples found in the remainder of this book are based upon many of these résumé writing and production principles. Examine those examples for ideas on how to develop each résumé section. But be sure **you write your own résumé** based upon the above principles rather than on the subsequent examples.

4

Evaluate Your Résumé Competence

Once you complete your résumé, be sure to evaluate it according to the principles outlined in Chapter 3. You should conduct two evaluations: internal and external. With an internal evaluation, you assess your résumé in reference to specific self-evaluation criteria. An external evaluation involves having someone else critique your résumé for its overall effectiveness.

Internal Evaluation

The first evaluation should take place immediately upon completing the first draft of your résumé. Examine your résumé in reference to the following evaluation criteria. Using the numerical ratings at the right, respond to each statement by circling the appropriate number that most accurately describes your new dynamite résumé:

1 = Strongly Agree
2 = Agree
3 = So-So
4 = Disagree
5 = Strongly Disagree

The numbers in parenthesis at the end of each statement correspond to each principle previously outlined in Chapter 3. Refer to these principles for further clarification.

WRITING

1. Wrote the résumé myself—no creative plagiarizing from others' résumé examples. (#1)   1   2   3   4   5

2. Conducted a thorough self-assessment which became the basis for writing each résumé section. (#1)   1   2   3   4   5

3. Have a plan of action that relates my résumé to other job search activities. (#2)   1   2   3   4   5

4. Selected an appropriate résumé format that best presents my interests, skills, and experience. (#3)   1   2   3   4   5

5. Included all essential information categories in the proper order. (#4-5)   1   2   3   4   5

6. Eliminated all extraneous information unrelated to my objective and employers' needs (date, picture, race, religion, political affiliation, age, sex, height, weight, marital status, health, hobbies) or better saved for discussion in the job interview—salary history and references. (#6)   1   2   3   4   5

7. Put the most important information first. (#5)   1   2   3   4   5

8. Résumé is oriented to the future rather than to the past. (#4)   1   2   3   4   5

9. Contact information is complete—name, address, and phone number. No P.O. Box numbers or nicknames. (#7 & #8)   1   2   3   4   5

10. Limited abbreviations to a few
    accepted words. (#8)   1   2   3   4   5

11. Contact information attractively
    formatted to introduce the résumé. (#8)   1   2   3   4   5

12. Included a thoughtful employer-oriented
    objective that incorporates both skills
    and benefits. (#9)   1   2   3   4   5

13. Objective clearly communicates to
    employers what I want to do, can do,
    and will do for them. (#9)   1   2   3   4   5

14. Objective is neither too general
    nor too specific. (#10)   1   2   3   4   5

15. Objective serves as the central
    organizing element for all other
    sections of the résumé. (#11)   1   2   3   4   5

16. Considered including a "Summary
    of Qualifications" section. (#12)   1   2   3   4   5

17. Elaborated work experience in detail,
    emphasizing my skills, abilities,
    and achievements. (#13 & #15)   1   2   3   4   5

18. Each "Experience" section is short
    and to the point. (#14)   1   2   3   4   5

19. Consistently used action verbs and
    the active voice. (#15-16)   1   2   3   4   5

20. Incorporates language appropriate
    for the keywords of electronic résumé
    scanners. (#17)   1   2   3   4   5

21. Did not refer to myself as "I". (#18)   1   2   3   4   5

22. Used specifics—numbers and percents—
    to highlight my performance. (#19)   1   2   3   4   5

23. Included positive quotations about my performance from previous employers. (#20)   1   2   3   4   5

24. Eliminated any negative references, including reasons for leaving. (#21)   1   2   3   4   5

25. Does not include names of supervisors. (#22)   1   2   3   4   5

26. Summarized my most recent job and then included other jobs in reverse chronological order. (#23)   1   2   3   4   5

27. Descriptions of "Experience" are consistent. (#24)   1   2   3   4   5

28. Put the most important information on my skills first when summarizing my "Experience." (#25)   1   2   3   4   5

29. No time gaps nor "job hopping" apparent to reader. (#26-27)   1   2   3   4   5

30. Documented "other experience" that might strengthen my objective and decided to either include or exclude it on the résumé. (#28)   1   2   3   4   5

31. Included complete information on my educational background, including important highlights. (#29)   1   2   3   4   5

32. If a recent graduate with little relevant work experience, emphasized educational background more than work experience. (#30)   1   2   3   4   5

33. Put education in reverse chronological order and eliminated high school if a college graduate. (#31)   1   2   3   4   5

34. Included special education and
    training relevant to my major
    interests and skills. (#32)   1   2   3   4   5

35. Included professional affiliations and
    memberships relevant to my objective
    and skills; highlighted any major
    contributions. (#33)   1   2   3   4   5

36. Documented any special skills not
    included elsewhere on résumé
    and included those that appear
    relevant to employers' needs. (#34)   1   2   3   4   5

37. Included awards or special recognitions
    that further document my skills and
    achievements. (#35)   1   2   3   4   5

38. Weighed pros and cons of including a
    personal statement on my résumé. (#36)   1   2   3   4   5

39. Did not mention salary history
    or expectations. (#37)   1   2   3   4   5

40. Did not include names, addresses,
    and phone number of references. (#38)   1   2   3   4   5

41. Included additional information to
    enhance the interest of employers. (#39)   1   2   3   4   5

42. Used a language appropriate for the
    employer, including terms that associate
    me with the industry. (#17 & #40)   1   2   3   4   5

43. My language is crisp, succinct,
    expressive, and direct. (#41)   1   2   3   4   5

44. Used emphasizing techniques to make
    the résumé most readable. (#42)   1   2   3   4   5

45. Selected language that is appropriate
    for being "read" by today's résumé
    scanning technology. (#43)   1   2   3   4   5

46. Résumé has an inviting, uncluttered look, incorporating sufficient white space and using a standard type style and size. (#44)   1   2   3   4   5

47. Kept the design very basic and conservative. (#45)   1   2   3   4   5

48. Kept sentences and sections short and succinct. (#46)   1   2   3   4   5

49. Résumé runs one or two pages. (#47)   1   2   3   4   5

PRODUCTION

50. Carefully proofread and produced two or three drafts which were subjected to both internal and external evaluations before producing the final copies. (#48)   1   2   3   4   5

51. Chose a standard color and quality of paper. (#49)   1   2   3   4   5

52. Used 8½ x 11" paper. (#50)   1   2   3   4   5

53. Printed résumé on only one side of paper. (#51)   1   2   3   4   5

54. Used a good quality machine and an easy-to-read typeface. (#52)   1   2   3   4   5

MARKETING AND DISTRIBUTION

55. Targeted résumé toward specific employers. (#53)   1   2   3   4   5

56. Used résumé properly for networking and informational interviewing activities. (#54)   1   2   3   4   5

57. Know how to properly send my résumé by e-mail.   1   2   3   4   5

58. Posted an electronic version of my
    résumé to several résumé databases
    operated by Internet employment sites
    as well as explored numerous bulletin
    boards, discussion groups, and employer
    sites on the Internet. (#53)   1   2   3   4   5

59. Résumé accompanied by a dynamite
    cover letter. (#54)   1   2   3   4   5

60. Only enclosed a cover letter with
    my résumé—nothing else. (#56)   1   2   3   4   5

61. Addressed to a specific name and
    position. (#57)   1   2   3   4   5

62. Mailed résumé and cover letter in
    a matching No. 10 business envelope
    or in a 9 x 12" envelope. (#58)   1   2   3   4   5

63. Typed address on envelope. (#59)   1   2   3   4   5

64. Sent correspondence by first-class
    or priority mail or special next-day
    services; affixed attractive
    commemorative stamps. (#60)   1   2   3   4   5

FOLLOW-UP

65. Followed-up the mailed résumé
    within 7 days. (#62)   1   2   3   4   5

66. Used the telephone for following
    up. (#63)   1   2   3   4   5

67. Followed-up the follow-up with
    a nice thank-you letter. (#64)   1   2   3   4   5

TOTAL

Add the numbers you circled to the right of each statement to get a cumulative score. If your score is higher than 90, you need to work on improving various aspects of your résumé. Go back and institute the necessary changes to create a truly dynamite résumé.

External Evaluation

In many respects the external résumé evaluation plays the most crucial role in your overall job search. It helps you get remembered which, in turn, leads to referrals and job leads.

The best way to conduct an external evaluation is to circulate your résumé to two or more individuals. Choose people whose opinions you value for being objective, frank, and thoughtful. Do not select friends and relatives who might flatter you with positive comments. Professional acquaintances or people you don't know personally but whom you admire may be good candidates for this type of evaluation.

An ideal evaluator has experience in hiring people in your area of expertise. In addition to sharing their experience with you, they may refer you to other individuals who would be interested in your qualifications. You will encounter many of these individuals in the process of networking and conducting informational interviews. You, in effect, conduct an external evaluation of your résumé with this individual during the informational interview. At the very end of the informational interview you should ask the person to examine your résumé; you want to elicit comments on how you can better strengthen the résumé. Ask him or her the following questions:

> *"If you don't mind, would you look over my résumé? Perhaps you could comment on its clarity or make suggestions for improving it?"*

> *"How would you react to this résumé if you received it from a candidate? Does it grab your attention and interest you enough to talk with me?"*

> *"If you were writing this résumé, what changes would you make? Any additions, deletions, or modifications?"*

Answers to these questions should give you invaluable feedback for improving both the form and content of your résumé. You will be eliciting advice from people whose opinions count. However, it is not necessary to incorporate all such advice. Some evaluators, while well-meaning, will not provide you with sound advice. Instead, they may reinforce many of the pitfalls found in weak résumés.

Another way to conduct an external evaluation is to develop a checklist of evaluation criteria and give it, along with your résumé, to individuals whose opinions and expertise you value. Unlike the evaluation criteria used for the internal evaluation, the evaluation criteria for the external evaluation should be more general. Examine your résumé in relation to these criteria:

Circle the number that best characterizes various aspects of my résumé as well as include any recommendations on how to best improve the résumé:

1 = Excellent
2 = Okay
3 = Weak

Recommendations for improvement

1. Overall appearance	1	2	3	_____
2. Layout	1	2	3	_____
3. Clarity	1	2	3	_____
4. Consistency	1	2	3	_____
5. Readability	1	2	3	_____
6. Language	1	2	3	_____
7. Organization	1	2	3	_____
8. Content/completeness	1	2	3	_____
9. Length	1	2	3	_____
10. Contact information/header	1	2	3	_____
11. Objective	1	2	3	_____
12. Experience	1	2	3	_____

13. Skills   1   2   3   _____

14. Achievements   1   2   3   _____

15. Education   1   2   3   _____

16. Other information   1   2   3   _____

17. Paper color   1   2   3   _____

18. Paper size and stock   1   2   3   _____

19. Overall production quality   1   2   3   _____

20. Potential effectiveness   1   2   3   _____

SUMMARY EVALUATION: _____

_____

_____

_____

_____

> As you'll quickly discover, your most effective job search strategy involves networking with your résumé.

After completing these external evaluations and incorporating useful suggestions for further improving the quality of your résumé, it's a good idea to send a copy of your revised résumé to those individuals who were helpful in giving you advice. Thank them for their time and thoughtful comments. Ask them to keep you in mind should they hear of anyone who might be interested in your experience and skills. In so doing, you will be demonstrating your appreciation and thoughtfulness as well as reminding them to remember you for further information, advice, and referrals.

In the end, **being remembered in reference to your résumé** is one of the most important goals you want to repeatedly achieve during your job search. As you will quickly discover, your most effective job search strategy involves networking with your résumé. You want to share information, by way of the informational interview, about your interests and qualifications with those who can give advice, know about job vacancies, or can refer you to individuals who have the power to hire. Your résumé, and especially this external evaluation, plays a critical role in furthering this process.

5

Transform an Ordinary Résumé
Into a Dynamite Résumé

M ost résumés can be improved by following several basic rules as outlined
in Chapter 3. If you already have a completed résumé, you should review
it in reference to the evaluation criteria outlined in Chapter 4.

Better still, let's look at four sets of examples that incorporate many
of our principles of effective résumé writing. These are actual examples from individuals who started with weak résumé writing skills and, with a little help, managed to transform an ordinary résumé into a dynamite résumé that led to interviews and job offers.

From Ordinary to Dynamite Résumés

Transforming an ordinary résumé into a dynamite résumé is not difficult if you keep focused on your purpose and incorporate a few basic principles of effective résumé writing. Indeed, after more than seventeen years of résumé writing, the single most important problem we have encountered with clients has been their inability to keep their writing, as well as their job search, **focused** on clear goals and purposes. They often wander aimlessly. The most important guiding principle is that your résumé should be **employer-centered** rather than self-centered. It should respond to the **needs of employers** rather than merely catalog your work history and express some interests. Everything you decide to put in your résumé, including each sentence and phrase you craft, must be done in reference to this principle. Keep everything focused around your purpose. You must separate those things that belong in a résumé from those things that are best discussed in a job interview, such as salary, references, reasons for leaving previous jobs, names of supervisors, or employment gaps. The résumé should be designed to generate positive responses about you as both a professional and an individual rather than raise and/or answer questions in a negative manner.

Always keep your résumé simple and focused on its purpose—**to elicit action on the part of the reader**. Like good advertising copy, you want to provide just enough interesting information to motivate your reader to take action. If you fail to keep this purpose in mind, you are likely to produce anything but a dynamite résumé.

> ❑ **Your résumé should be employer-centered rather than self-centered.**
>
> ❑ **Keep everything on your résumé focused around your purpose.**
>
> ❑ **You must separate those things that belong in a résumé from those things that are best discussed in a job interview.**
>
> ❑ **Like good advertising copy, your résumé should provide just enough information to motivate the reader to take action.**

If written properly, your résumé will begin taking on a life of its own. It will capsulize in one page what exactly you:

- **Want to do:** a statement of your goals and objectives.

- **Can do:** statements of your actual performance.

- **Will do in the future:** a probability conclusion drawn by the reader based upon a summary analysis of your résumé content.

It should clearly address the needs of employers. You do this by answering the key questions employers ask concerning you in reference to your résumé:

- What can this person do for me?

- How will this person fit into our organization?

- Will this person be able to solve our problems and grow within our organization?

- Should I contact this person for an interview to answer several other equally important questions?

The following résumé transformations speak to these principles. Primarily focusing on the needs of employers rather than the interests of the résumé writer, each résumé should be viewed as a concerted effort to **motivate employers to take action**—invite the résumé writer to a job interview.

Gail Topper

The first case, Gail Topper (page 87), is an actual case study. While it is not a typical case, it does emphasize how to handle important employment problems with different types of résumés. The individual had held several full-time positions as typist, secretary, receptionist, and sales clerk while working her way through college. After graduation, she continued in her former occupation. Wanting to break out of the "once a secretary, always a secretary" pattern, she has several résumé options for changing careers. Everything appearing here is true. One of the major differences is the truth is better communicated to her advantage in some résumés than in others.

Traditional Chronological Résumé

Résumé

Gail S. Topper
136 W. Davis St.
Washington, DC 20030
202-465-9821

Weight:	122 lbs.
Height:	5'4"
Born:	8/4/60
Health:	Good
Marital Status:	Married

Education

1986-1993   George Mason University, Fairfax, Virginia. I received my B.A. in Comunications.

1983-1985   Northern Virginia Community College, Annandale, Virginia. I completed my A.A. degree.

1978-1982   Harrisonburg High School, Harrisonburg, Virginia.

Work Experience

2/14/92 to present: Secretary, MCT Coporation, 2381 Rhode Island Ave., Philadelphia, Pennsylvania 19322.

2/30/90 to 2/9/92: Secretary, Martin Computer Services, 391 Old Main Rd., Charleston, South Carolina 37891.

4/21/89 to 2/20/90: Secretary, STR Systems, Inc., 442 Virginia Ave., Rm. 21, Washington, D.C. 20011.

9/28/88 to 1/4/89: Typist, NTC Corporation, 992 Fairy Avenue, Springfield, Virginia 22451.

1/9/88 to 7/30/88: Secretary, Foreign Language Department, George Mason University, Fairfax, Virginia 22819

3/1/86 to 9/14/87: Salesclerk, Sears Reobuck & Co., 294 Wisconsin Avenue, Boston, Massachusetts 08233

5/3/83 to 2/1/85: Salesclerk, JT's, 332 Monroe St., New Orleans, Louisiana 70014.

1978-1982: Held several jobs as cook, counter help, salesclerk, typist, and secretarial assistant.

Community Involvement

1993 to prsent: Sunday school teacher. Grace Methodist Church. Falls Church, Virginia.

1989: Volunteer. Red Cross. Falls Church, Virginia.

1985: Stage crew member. Community Theatre Group.
New Orleans, Louisiana

1984: Extra. Community Theatre Group. Annandale, Virginia.

Hobbies

I like to swim, cook, garden, bicycle, and listen to rock music.

Personal Statement

I have good mannual dexterity developed by working back stage in theatrical productions and working with various office machines. I can operate IBM Mag Card A and II typeriters, dictaphones, IBM 6640 (ink jet printer), various duplicating machines, and several copying machines. Familiar with addressograph. I am willing to relocate nad travel.

References

John R. Teems, Manager, Martin Computer Services, 391 Old Dominion Rd., Annandale, Virginia 20789

James Stevens, Secretary, STR Systems, Inc., 442 Virginia Ave., Rm. 21, Washington, D.C. 20011.

Alice Bears, Assistant Personnel Director, MCT Corporation, 2381 Rhode Island Ave., Philadelphia, Pennsylvania 19322

Also contact the Office of Career Planning and Placement at George Mason University.

The first résumé represents the **traditional chronological or "obituary" résumé**. It stresses skills and accomplishments in relationship to an objective. The writer presents jobs that don't strengthen her objective.

The **improved chronological résumé** on page 96 presents a totally different picture of Gail Topper. It stresses skills and accomplishments in relationship to an objective. She presents jobs with supports that strengthen her objective.

The **functional résumé** on page 94 presents another picture of this individual's qualifications. Here, employment dates and job titles are eliminated in favor of presenting transferable skills and accomplishments. While this résumé is ideal for someone entering the job market with little job related experience, this résumé does not take advantage of this individual's work experience with specific employers.

The **combination résumé** on page 95 is ideal for this particular person. It minimizes employment dates and job titles, stresses transferable skills and accomplishments, and includes work history. Here, the individual appears purposeful, skilled, and experienced.

The résumé letter on page 96 also is a good alternative for this person in lieu of the traditional résumé. The individual can present a résumé—preferably the combination résumé—to the employer at some later date.

Notice the secretarial experience does not appear on the improved chronological, functional, or combination résumés. If it did, it would tend to stereotype this individual prior to being invited to an interview. It is important, however, that this individual be able to explain the secretarial experience during the interview, especially how it will make her a particularly good salesperson—knows the particular equipment and problems from the perspective of those who will use it on a day-to-day basis.

This individual was pleased with her chronological résumé—she thought it outlined a great deal of education and work experience that would appeal to potential employers. However, if you examine this résumé carefully, you will notice this individual violated several principles of good résumé writing. First, she includes a great deal of **extraneous information**, beginning with weight, height, age, health, and marital status in the header to including irrelevant hobbies as well as names and addresses of references. None of this information relates to any bonafide hiring criteria. It distracts from the résumé as well as raises possible negative questions.

This résumé also clearly **lacks a focus**. Worst of all, it **raises many negative questions and conclusions** about the individual's goals, interests, and employment history. Remember, employers look for **patterns of work behavior** that will provide clues about the individual's **probable future**

performance. Three unflattering patterns are apparent from this résumé:

- She appears to be a job-hopper.

- She's someone with an unfocused career.

- She's an educated secretary/typist with a communication major who makes spelling mistakes!

Based on previous experience, the employer also might conclude this is possibly someone with low self-esteem.

An employer reading this résumé is likely to raise these negative questions and draw several negative conclusions:

- What is it she wants to do?

- What useful skills will she bring to our organization?

- Why has she changed jobs so often?

- Maybe she's a secretary, but she could be a salesclerk, a typist, or a computer operator. Her occupational profile is unclear.

- Can't spell! I wonder what else she can't do.

- I think she'll leave her next job within a few months. I wouldn't give her more than a year in our organization.

- I don't want to waste my time on this one. She spells trouble!

You should never have such negative questions raised nor conclusions drawn about you based on your résumé. This is truly an obituary résumé, destined to join the graveyard of so many other ineffective résumés.

This résumé has numerous problems, but the most serious problem is found in the **choice of résumé format**. Remember, résumé format helps structure one's thinking about an individual's qualifications. Moreover, you always want to put your most important information first. If you present dates first, you invite the reader to analyze your résumé chronologically and thus ask chronological questions. The reader will begin looking for time gaps as well as average length of employment with each employer.

Gail Topper obviously has a checkered employment history when she presents her experience in chronological terms. Unfortunately, employment dates were her weakest point but she presented them initially and thus did just the opposite of what she should have done—presented her weakest points first! In fact, the reason for making so many job changes was her family situation—her husband was in the U.S. Navy and was transferred often—something employers would not know except in a job interview after asking "Why did you leave your job at companies A, B, C, D, and E?" Since she will never get to the interview stage with most employers, she let the reader raise a negative question then intuitively answer it:

> "Why did she change jobs so often. She's probably an unstable employee who may lack good work habits. We don't need to hire this problem!"

The reality is that she took sales, typing, and secretarial jobs because she was unable to build a career in such a mobile family situation. These jobs actually accentuated her weaknesses—regardless of all her education and training, she couldn't spell! She was dyslexic. She had excellent skills, many unrelated to secretarial work, and was an outstanding worker. But Uncle Sam called her husband to often pack up and move to another military installation. When looking for new employment, she managed to always shoot herself in the foot with this type of résumé. Her biggest problem was in putting all her experience into a traditional chronological format which further accentuated her unstable work history and communicated low value to potential employers.

There were other ways she could have presented her qualifications to employers, but she didn't know how to do it. In fact, she thought she already had a good résumé—she had used other examples as the basis for writing her own résumé rather than generate important job and career information on herself. The first thing she needed to do was to undergo a complete self-assessment for identifying her major interests, skills, and abilities. She needed this information in order to focus her résumé around an objective and to develop an appropriate language—using action verbs and the active voice—for writing each résumé section. Since her employment dates were her weakest points, she had to abandon the traditional chronological résumé in favor of other résumé formats that could better present her strongest qualifications first.

The process of transforming this résumé in reality also became a process of self-discovery. It was a personal journey into the world of career planning which involves such issues as self-esteem, identifying interests and values, charting goals, specifying achievements, and planning for the next ten years of her worklife. She went through both a personal and professional transformation; she learned a great deal about herself—her goals, interests, skills, and abilities which were previously buried under the irrelevant baggage of the traditional chronological résumé. Above all, she discovered she was pursuing her career weaknesses (remember, she can't spell!) rather than her strengths which she had yet to systematically identify. In other words, she had been in all the wrong jobs most of her adult working life.

In the process of creating a new résumé, she literally transformed her whole job and career orientation. Indeed, the résumé writing exercise became an important transformation in her life. The good news is that she has found terrific jobs ever since! Her husband, who has since retired from the U.S. Navy, has also applied the same principles in writing his own dynamite résumé which has resulted in similar career success.

After much soul searching centered on identifying her major strengths—motivated abilities and skills (MAS)—we were able to point her in more fruitful career directions that emphasized what was **right** about her. She developed a new résumé with a new career objective which was supported by patterns of skills and accomplishments. Moving away from the traditional chronological résumé, which was inappropriate given her background and career interests, we developed four different types of résumés using other résumé formats: Improved Chronological, Functional, Combination, and Résumé Letter. Examine each of these examples carefully on pages 96-99. Keep in mind that everything in these résumés is true, but we've been able to refocus this person's life around clear goals, patterns of accomplishments, and the needs of employers. You will quickly see that this person has many **strengths** that were not apparent from reading her Traditional Chronological Résumé.

Improved Chronological Résumé

GAIL S. TOPPER
136 West Davis Street
Washington, DC 20030   202/465-9821

OBJECTIVE: A professional sales position. . . leading to management. . . in information processing where administrative and technical experience, initiative, and interpersonal skills will be used for maximizing sales and promoting good customer relations.

EDUCATION: **B.A. in Communication, 1989**
George Mason University, Fairfax, Virginia.
- Courses in interpersonal communication, psychology, and public speaking.
- Worked full-time in earning 100% of educational and personal expenses.

TECHNICAL EXPERIENCE: **MCT Corporation, 2381 Rhode Island Avenue, Philadelphia, PA 20033:** Office management and materials production responsibilities. Planned and re-organized word processing center. Initiated time and cost studies, which saved company $30,000 in additional labor costs. Improved efficiency of personnel. 1992 to present.

Martin Computer Services, 391 Main Rd., Charleston, SC 37891: Communication and materials production responsibilities. Handled customer complaints. Created new tracking and filing system for Mag cards. Improved turnaround time for documents production. Operated Savin word processor. 1990 to 1992.

STR Systems, 442 Virginia Avenue, Rm. 21, Washington, DC 20011: Equipment operation and production responsibilities. Operated Mag card and high speed printers: IBM 6240, Mag A,I,II,IBM 6640. Developed and organized technical reference room for more effective use of equipment. 1989-1990.

SALES EXPERIENCE: **Sears Roebuck & Co., 294 Wisconsin Avenue, Boston, MA 08233:** Promoted improved community relations with company. Solved customer complaints. Reorganized product displays. Handled orders. 1986 to 1988.

JT's, 332 Monroe St., New Orleans, LA 70014: Recruited new clients. Maintained inventory. Developed direct sales approach. 1983 to 1985.

Functional Résumé

GAIL S. TOPPER

136 West Davis St.	Washington, DC 20030	202/465-9821

OBJECTIVE: A professional sales position. . .leading to management. . . in information processing where administrative and technical experience, initiative, and interpersonal skills will be used for maximizing sales and promoting good customer relations.

EDUCATION: **B.A. in Communication, 1990**
George Mason University, Fairfax, Virginia.
- Courses in interpersonal communication, psychology, and public speaking.
- Worked full-time in earning 100% of educational and personal expenses.

AREAS OF EFFECTIVENESS

SALES/ CUSTOMER RELATIONS: Promoted improved community relations with business. Solved customer complaints. Recruited new clients. Re-organized product displays. Maintained inventory. Received and filled orders.

PLANNING/ ORGANIZING: Planned and re-organized word processing center. Initiated time and cost studies, which saved company additional labor costs and improved efficiency of personnel. Developed and organized technical reference room for more effective utilization of equipment. Created new tracking and filing system for Mag cards which resulted in eliminating redundancy and improving turnaround time.

TECHNICAL: Eight years of experience in operating Mag card and high speed printers: IBM 6240, Mag A, I,II,IBM 6640, and Savin word processor.

PERSONAL: 30. . .excellent health. . .enjoy challenges. . .interested in productivity. . .willing to relocate and travel.

REFERENCES: Available upon request.

Combination Résumé

GAIL S. TOPPER

136 West Davis St.   Washington, DC 20030   202/465-9821

OBJECTIVE: A professional sales position. . .leading to management. . . in information processing where administrative and technical experience, initiative, and interpersonal skills will be used for maximizing sales and promoting good customer relations.

AREAS OF EFFECTIVENESS

SALES/ CUSTOMER RELATIONS: Promoted improved community relations with business. Solved customer complaints. Recruited new clients. Re-organized product displays. Maintained inventory. Received and filled orders.

PLANNING/ ORGANIZING   Planned and re-organized word processing center. Initiated time and cost studies, which saved company additional labor costs and improved efficiency of personnel. Developed and organized technical reference room for more effective utilization of equipment. Created new tracking and filing system for Mag cards which resulted in eliminating redundancy and improving turnaround time.

TECHNICAL: Eight years of experience in operating Mag card and high speed printers: IBM 6240, Mag A,I,II,IBM 6640, and Savin word processor.

EMPLOYMENT EXPERIENCE: MCT Corporation, Philadelphia, PA
Martin Computer Services, Charleston, SC
STR Systems, Inc., Washington, DC
NTC Corporation, Springfield, VA

EDUCATION: **B.A. in Communication, 1990**
George Mason University, Fairfax, Virginia.
- Courses in interpersonal communication, psychology, and public speaking.
- Worked full-time in earning 100% of educational and personal expenses.

PERSONAL: 30. . .excellent health. . .enjoy challenges. . .interested in productivity. . .willing to relocate and travel.

Résumé Letter

136 W. Davis St.
Washington, DC 20030
January 7, _____

James C. Thomas, President
Advanced Technology Corporation
721 West Stevens Road
Bethesda, MD 20110

Dear Mr. Thomas:

Advanced Technology's word processing equipment is the finest on the market today. I know because I have used different systems over the past eight years. Your company is the type of organization I would like to be associated with.

Over the next few months I will be seeking a sales position with an information processing company. My technical, sales, and administrative experience include:

- Technical: eight years operating Mag card and high speed printers: IBM 6240, MAG A,I,II,IBM 6640, and Savin word processor.

- Sales: recruited clients; maintained inventory; received and filled orders; improved business-community relations.

- Administrative: planned and re-organized word processing center; created new tracking and filing systems; initiated time and cost studies which reduced labor costs by $30,000 and improved efficiency of operations.

In addition, I have a bachelor's degree in communication with emphasis on public speaking, interpersonal communication, and psychology.

Your company interests me very much. I would appreciate an opportunity to meet with you to discuss how my qualifications can best meet your needs. I will call your office next Monday, January 18, to arrange a meeting with you at a convenient time.

Thank you for your consideration.

Sincerely yours,

Gail S. Topper

Gail S. Topper

Karen Jones

The second set of examples (pages 98-103) relates to a situation faced by thousands of educators each year—making a career transition from education to some other occupational field. These résumés also are relevant to millions of other individuals who decide to make career changes at some point in their worklives. The question facing them is how to best present their past work history which is not directly related to jobs held in another career field. How can you appear qualified when you don't have direct work experience in the other field? The secret is to focus on **transferable skills**—those skills which are common in many different occupational fields—and then present them in an appropriate résumé format that will stress the particular talents of the career changer. We apply this strategy in this set of examples.

In these examples, our subject, Karen Jones, begins with the Traditional Chronological Résumé and transforms it into an Improved Chronological, Functional, and Combination résumé as well as a Résumé Letter. Each résumé format tends to emphasize different aspects of her qualifications. For example, the Traditional Chronological Résumé on pages 98-99 basically tells prospective employers that she is a teacher without career goals. It lacks an objective, includes extraneous information, and lists work history by dates. Accentuating her negatives, this is an inappropriate résumé for such a career changer.

The Improved Chronological Résumé on page 100 gives us a clearer picture of what she wants to do as well as what she has done in the past. However, it still emphasizes the fact that she is a former teacher. This format does not enable her to emphasize those skills that are most relevant to her objective. Nonetheless, this is a great improvement over her Traditional Chronological Résumé.

The Functional, Combination, and Letter résumés on pages 101-103 enable Karen Jones to better demonstrate her transferable skills in relation to a desired non-teaching position. Any of these résumé formats would be most appropriate for someone making a significant career change.

Traditional Chronological Résumé

Karen Jones

Address: 1234 Main Street
                  Norfolk, VA 23508

Telephone: Area Code 804, Number 440-4321

Marital Status: Divorced; 2 children; ages 10 and 12
Date of Birth: April 1, 1958
Health: Excellent
Height: 5 feet, 4 inches
Weight: 125 lbs.

Educational Background:

University of Virginia, Charlottesville, Virginia. Bachelor of Arts Degree in English Literature with Certification in Secondary Education, June 1980.

Old Dominion University, Norfolk, Virginia. Master of Science Degree in Secondary Education, June 1985.

Work History:

1986 to Present—Norfolk Public Schools, Norfolk, VA.
English Teacher—I teach 11th and 12th grade English composition and creative writing classes. I have also served as co-director of the senior class play, coordinated student fund raising activities, and chaired the school committee which developed recruiting and public relations materials. I have given speeches at student events and helped write speeches for the school administration.

1981-1986—Full-time Homemaker.

1993-1981—Chesapeake Public Schools, Chesapeake, Virginia.
English Teacher—I taught 10th and 11th grade composition classes.

Community Involvements:

Toastmaster's International. Since 1985, I have been very active and have held a variety of chapter offices. During the past three years I have served as a district representative and officer.

Hobbies and Interests:

I enjoy physical exercise (running and racquetball), sailing, piano, theater, gardening, and gourmet cooking.

References:

Dr. James Smith, Superintendent of Norfolk Public Schools.
Mr. Robert Sinclair, Principal, Norfolk High School.
Mr. Paul Amos, Governor, Tidewater District, Toastmasters International.

Improved Chronological Résumé

KAREN JONES
1234 Main Street
Norfolk, VA 23508
804/440-4321

OBJECTIVE: A public relations position involving program planning and coordination which requires an ability to work with diverse publics, develop publicity and promotional campaigns, market services and benefits, and meet deadlines.

WORK EXPERIENCE:

English Teacher: Norfolk Public Schools, Norfolk, VA.
Taught creative writing and composition. Organized and supervised numerous fund-raising projects which involved local businesses, media, parents, and students. Co-directed senior class plays. Wrote and gave several "keynote" speeches at special student programs. Served as school liaison to Parent-Teachers Association; designed a plan to increase membership and involve parents in school activities. Chaired city-wide public relations committee; coordinated development and production of promotional materials. Served as speech "ghost-writer" and editor for administrators. (1986 to present)

English Teacher: Chesapeake Public Schools, Chesapeake, VA.
Taught English composition. Wrote, designed, and developed multimedia instructional programs to interest students in writing. Served as advisor to student newspaper. (1979-1981)

ADDITIONAL EXPERIENCE:

Toastmasters International, Tidewater Chapter, VA.

District Representative: Elected to governing board of Southeast Virginia District. Served in liaison capacity between district officers and local chapter. Planned, organized, and publicized training workshops and regional competition. (1992 to present).

Chapter Officer (President, Treasurer, Sergeant-at-Arms):
Developed a publicity plan which increased membership by 20 percent. Kept financial records and prepared budget reports. Acquired extensive public speaking experience and training. (1988-1995)

EDUCATION:

M.S.Ed. in Secondary Education, 1985: Old Dominion University, Norfolk, VA
B.A. in English Literature, 1981: University of Virginia, Charlottesville, VA

Functional Résumé

KAREN JONES
1234 Main Street
Norfolk, VA 23508
804/440-4321

OBJECTIVE:	A public relations position involving program planning and coordination which requires an ability to work with diverse publics, develop publicity and promotional campaigns, market services and benefits, and meet deadlines.

AREAS OF EFFECTIVENESS

PLANNING AND COORDINATING	Organized and supervised several fund raising projects. Designed and implemented membership campaigns. Chaired public relations committee for school system; coordinated development and production of promotional materials. Publicized special events and pro grams to constituent groups. Developed multi-media instructional package to facilitate learning and involve students. Taught creative writing.
PROMOTING PUBLICIZING, MARKETING, AND WRITING	Developed promotional plan to attract new members to organizations. Coordinated publicity of special events and media. Wrote and edited speeches for self and school administrators. Helped design and produce pro motional materials. Publicized special events and programs to constituent groups. Developed multi-media instructional package to facilitate learning and involve students. Taught creative writing.
COMMUNICATING AND INSTRUCTING	Gave numerous speeches over a seven year period to a variety of audiences. Conducted meetings and chaired committees. Coached administrators in writing and presenting speeches. Taught English for ten years in public schools.
EDUCATION:	M.S.Ed., Old Dominion University, Norfolk, VA, 1985. B.A., University of Virginia, Charlottesville, VA, 1980.

Combination Résumé

KAREN JONES
1234 Main Street
Norfolk, VA 23508
804/440-4321

OBJECTIVE: A public relations position involving program planning and coordination which requires an ability to work with diverse publics, develop publicity and promotional campaigns, market services and benefits, and meet deadlines.

AREAS OF EFFECTIVENESS

PLANNING COORDINATING

Organized and supervised several fund raising projects. Designed and implemented membership campaigns. Chaired public relations committee for school system; coordinated development and production of promotional materials. Publicized special events and programs to constituent groups. Developed multi-media instructional package to facilitate learning and involve students. Taught creative writing.

PROMOTING PUBLICIZING, MARKETING, AND WRITING

Developed promotional plan to attract new members to organizations. Coordinated publicity of special events and media. Wrote and edited speeches for self and school administrators. Helped design and produce pro motional materials. Publicized special events and programs to constituent groups. Developed multi-media instructional package to facilitate learning and involve students. Taught creative writing.

COMMUNICATING AND INSTRUCTING

Gave numerous speeches over a seven year period to a variety of audiences. Conducted meetings and chaired committees. Coached administrators in writing and presenting speeches. Taught English for ten years.

WORK EXPERIENCE:

English Teacher: Norfolk Public Schools, Norfolk, VA.
11th and 12th grade creative writing and composition. (1986-present)

English Teacher: Chesapeake Public Schools, Chesapeake, VA.
10th and 11th grade composition. Advisor to student newspaper. (1979-1981).

EDUCATION:

M.S.Ed., Old Dominion University, Norfolk, VA, 1985.
B.A., University of Virginia, Charlottesville, VA, 1979.

Résumé Letter

1234 Main Street
Norfolk, VA 23508
April 30, _____

Mr. Dale Roberts
Business Manager
Virginia Beach Convention Center
Virginia Beach, VA 23519

Dear Mr. Roberts:

A mutual acquaintance of ours, Paul Amos, suggested that I contact you about the new Virginia Beach Convention Center. He remarked that you are developing a comprehensive public relations and marketing plan to attract convention business.

As an officer of my local chapter and regional division of Toastmasters International, I have acquired a substantial amount of public relations, special events planning, and program coordination experience. Along with my professional work, my background includes working with diverse audiences, developing publicity campaign and promotional materials, marketing services and benefits, recruiting new members, handling financial records, and meeting important deadlines. Furthermore, I have experience in writing and giving speeches, chairing work groups, representing organizations, creative writing, and teaching.

Since I have a strong interest in public relations-type activities and have a thorough knowledge of our region and its resources, I was quite interested to hear that your new marketing plan may use conference coordinators to work with your sales staff. I would be very interested in learning more about your plans and exploring future possibilities.

I plan to be near your office next week and wonder if we could have a brief meeting? I'll give your office a call in the next few days to see if a mutually convenient time could be arranged.

Sincerely,

Karen Jones

Karen Jones

James C. Astor

Our third set of examples follows a similar pattern—transforming a Traditional Chronological Résumé into Improved Chronological, Functional, Combination, and Letter résumés. In this case, the individual has a background in counseling and training. He seeks to move from public sector employment to a private firm. He was actually terminated from his last government job due to budgetary cutbacks that eliminated his position. This is the first time he has had to write a one-page résumé appropriate for the private sector—and he manages to incorporate numerous errors associated with résumé writing.

Notice, again, how we take what is essentially a weak self-centered résumé filled with potential negatives and transform it into a coherent résumé. The new résumés incorporate the individual's major skills and accomplishments as well as target them toward the needs of employers. Take special note of the Combination Résumé example. Here we extend the basic one-page résumé to a second "Supplemental Information" page. This is a good alternative to writing a two-page résumé. The "Supplemental Information" page summarizes major achievements that are best pulled together in this format rather than incorporated into the "Experience" section of the first page.

Traditional Chronological Résumé

Résumé

James C. Astor
4921 Taylor Drive
Washington, D.C. 20011

Weight:	190 lbs.
Height:	6'0"
Born:	June 2, 1960
Health:	Good
Marital Status:	Divorced

EDUCATION

1989-1990: M.A., Vocational Counseling, Virginia Commonwealth University, Richmond, Virginia.

1978-1982: B.A., Psychology, Roanoke College, Salem, Virginia.

1974-1978: High School Diploma, Richmond Community High School, Richmond, Virginia.

WORK EXPERIENCE

6/13/90 to 8/22/97: Supervisory Trainer, GS-12, U.S. Department of Labor, Washington, D.C. Responsible for all aspects of training. Terminated because of budget cuts.

9/10/88 to 11/21/89: Bartender, Johnnie's Disco, Richmond, Virginia. Part-time while attending college.

4/3/86 to 6/2/88; Counselor, Virginia Employment Commission, Richmond, Virginia. Responsible for interviewing unemployed for jobs. Resigned to work full-time on Master's degree.

8/15/83 to 6/15/85: Guidance counselor and teacher, Petersburg Junior High School, Petersburg, Virginia.

2/11/81 to 10/6/81: Cook and Waiter, Big Mama's Pizza Parlor, Roanoke, Virginia. Part-time while attending college.

PROFESSIONAL AFFILIATIONS

American Personnel and Guidance Association
American Society for Training and Development
Personnel Management Association
Phi Delta Pi

HOBBIES

I like to play tennis, bicycle, and hike.

REFERENCES

David Ryan, Chief, Training Division, U.S. Department of Labor, Washington, D.C. 20012, (202) 735-0121.

Dr. Sara Thomas, Professor, Department of Psychology, George Washington University, Washington, D.C. 20030, (201) 621-4545.

Thomas V. Grant, Area Manager, Virginia Employment Commission, Richmond, Virginia 26412, (804) 261-4089

Improved Chronological Résumé

JAMES C. ASTOR
4921 Tyler Drive
Washington, DC 20011   212/422-8764

OBJECTIVE: A training and counseling position with a computer firm, where strong administrative, communication, and planning abilities will be used for improving the work performance and job satisfaction of employees.

EXPERIENCE: **U.S. Department of Labor, Washington, DC**
Planned and organized counseling programs for 5,000 employees. Developed training manuals and conducted workshops on interpersonal skills, stress management, and career planning; resulted in a 50 percent decrease in absenteeism. Supervised team of five instructors and counselors. Conducted individual counseling and referrals to community organizations. Advised government agencies and private firms on establishing in-house employee counseling and career development programs. Consistently evaluated as outstanding by supervisors and workshop participants. 1990 to present.

Virginia Employment Commission, Richmond, VA
Conducted all aspects of employment counseling. Interviewed, screened, and counseled 2,500 jobseekers. referred clients to employers and other agencies. Coordinated job vacancy and training information for businesses, industries, and schools. Reorganized interviewing and screening processes which improved the efficiency of operations by 50 percent. Cited in annual evaluation for "outstanding contributions to improving relations with employers and clients." 1986-1988.

Petersburg Junior High School, Petersburg, VA
Guidance counselor for 800 students. Developed program of individualized and group counseling. Taught special social science classes for socially maladjusted and slow learners. 1983-1985.

EDUCATION: M.A., Vocational Counseling, Virginia Commonwealth University, Richmond, VA, 1990.

B.A., Psychology, Roanoke College, Salem, VA, 1982.

REFERENCES: Available upon request.

Functional Résumé

JAMES C. ASTOR

4921 Tyler Drive	Washington, DC 20011	212/422-8764

OBJECTIVE: A training and counseling position with a computer firm, where strong administrative, communication, and planning abilities will be used for improving the work performance and job satisfaction of employees.

EDUCATION: Ph.D. in process, Industrial Psychology, George Washington University, Washington, DC

M.A., Vocational Counseling, Virginia Commonwealth University, Richmond, VA, 1990.

B.A., Psychology, Roanoke College, Salem, VA, 1982.

AREAS OF EFFECTIVENESS:

Administration

Supervised instructors and counselors. Coordinated job vacancy and training information for businesses, industries, and schools.

Communication

Conducted over 100 workshops on interpersonal skills, stress management, and career planning. Frequent guest speaker to various agencies and private firms. Experienced writer of training manuals and public relations materials.

Planning

Planned and developed counseling programs for 5,000 employees. Reorganized interviewing and screening processes for public employment agency. Developed program of individualized and group counseling for community school.

PERSONAL: Enjoy challenges and working with people. . .interested in productivity. . .willing to relocate and travel.

REFERENCES: Available upon request.

Combination Résumé

JAMES C. ASTOR
4921 Tyler Drive
Washington, DC 20011   212/422-8764

OBJECTIVE: A training and counseling position with a computer firm, where strong administrative, communication, and planning abilities will be used for improving the work performance and job satisfaction of employees.

AREAS OF EFFECTIVENESS

ADMINISTRATION: Supervised instructors and counselors. Coordinated job vacancy and training information for businesses, industries, and schools.

COMMUNICATION: Conducted over 100 workshops on interpersonal skills, stress management, and career planning. Frequent guest speaker to various agencies and private firms. Experienced writer of training manuals and public relations materials.

PLANNING: Planned and developed counseling programs for 5,000 employees. Reorganized interviewing and screening processes for public employment agency. Developed program of individualized and group counseling for community school.

WORK HISTORY: Supervisory Trainer, U.S. Department of Labor, Washington, DC, 1994 to present.

Counselor, Virginia Employment Commission, Richmond, VA, 1990-1992.

Guidance counselor and teacher, Petersburg Junior High School, Petersburg, VA, 1987-1989.

EDUCATION: M.A., Vocational Counseling, Virginia Commonwealth University, Richmond, VA, 1994.

B.A., Psychology, Roanoke College, Salem, VA, 1986.

PERSONAL: Enjoy challenges and working with people . . . interested in productivity . . . willing to relocate and travel.

SUPPLEMENTAL INFORMATION   JAMES C. ASTOR

Continuing Education and Training

- Completed 12 semester hours of computer science courses.
- Attended several workshops during past three years on employee counseling and administrative methods:

  "Career Development for Technical Personnel," Professional Management Association, 3 days, 1999.

  "Effective Supervisory Methods for Training Directors," National Training Associates, 3 days, 1998.

  "Training the Trainer," American Society for Training and Development, 3 days, 1997.

  "Time Management," U.S. Department of Labor, 3 days, 1996.

  "Counseling the Substance Abuse Employee," American Management Association, 3 days, 1995.

Training Manuals Developed

- "Managing Employee Stress," U.S. Department of Labor, 1998.
- "Effective Interpersonal Communication in the Workplace," U.S. Department of Labor, 1997.
- "Planning Careers Within the Organization," U.S. Department of Labor, 1996.

Research Projects Completed

- "Employment Counseling Programs for Technical Personnel," U.S. Development of Labor, 1999. Incorporated into agency report on "New Directions in Employee Counseling."
- "Developing Training Programs for Problem Employees," M.A. thesis, Virginia Commonwealth University, 1996.

Professional Affiliations

- American Personnel and Guidance Association
- American Society for Training and Development
- Personnel Management Association

Educational Highlights

- Completing Ph.D. in Industrial Psychology, George Washington University, Washington, D.C.
- Earned 4.0/4.0 grade point average as graduate student.
- Organized the Graduate Student Counseling Association for George Washington University, 1996.

Résumé Letter

4921 Tyler Drive
Washington, DC 20011

March 15, _____

Doris Stevens
STR Corporation
179 South Trail
Rockville, MD 21101

Dear Ms. Stevens:

STR Corporation is one of the most dynamic computer companies in the nation. In addition to being a leader in the field of small business computers, STR has a progressive employee training and development program which could very well become a model for other organizations. This is the type of organization I am interested in joining.

I am seeking a training position with a computer firm which would use my administrative, communication, and planning abilities to develop effective training and counseling programs. My experience includes:

Administration: Supervised instructors and counselors. Coordinated job vacancy and training information for businesses, industries, and schools.

Communication: Conducted over 100 workshops on interpersonal skills, stress management, and career planning. Frequent guest speaker to various agencies and private firms. Experienced writer of training manuals and public relations materials.

Planning: Planned and developed counseling programs for 5,000 employees. Reorganized interviewing and screening processes for public employment agency. Developed program of individualized and group counseling for community school.

In addition, I am completing my Ph.D. in industrial psychology with emphasis on developing training and counseling programs for technical personnel.

Could we meet to discuss your program as well as how my experience might relate to your needs? I will call your office on Tuesday morning, March 23, to arrange a convenient time to meet with you.

I especially want to share with you a model employee counseling and career development program I recently developed. Perhaps you may find it useful for your work with STR.

Sincerely,

James Astor

James Astor

George Willington

Because of our international work, we receive numerous inquiries from individuals who seek international employment. Some individuals have many years of experience working abroad. Others wish to re-enter the international job market after a lengthy absence. And others wish to break into this job market with little or no experience nor marketable international skills. Unfortunately, we hear from a disproportionate number of individuals who are high on motivation to work abroad but very low on international skills and experience and knowledge of international employers and jobs. Many are construction workers who have unrealistic expectations about the marketability of their skills abroad. Indeed, this is the job market for many dreamers who see themselves making tons of money working in some exotic location. It is also a job market for individuals who seriously pursue international careers based upon a sound understanding of the realities of the international job market. In either case, they need a résumé that best communicates their qualifications to international employers.

The final set of résumé transformation examples are different from the previous examples. Here we show how to change an objective for two different employment arenas—international and domestic—as well as how to move from a self-employed situation to that of employee in someone else's organization. It incorporates the interests of a talented individual who is interested in pursuing many different professional and personal interests which cannot be accommodated in a single job. While he may appear to lack a clear focus—doesn't seem to know what he wants to do—he really wants to do many different things, all of which present new career challenges. So he takes it one job at a time. Whichever job falls in line will be the one he will enjoy.

This individual has a strong professional background in both architecture and construction as well as a personal interest in international travel and work. He also has an interesting personal/professional background that includes technical and writing skills and travel/relocation interests—interesting enough to be included in "Additional Skills and Experience" and "Personal" sections. These additional skills and interests give his résumé personality. They set him apart from many other applicants. In the end, they may be the real reason employers invite him to interviews.

Most of George Willington's experience is as an independent contractor rather than as an employee in someone else's organization. He's interested in using his professional skills in either the United States or abroad. However, if he is to appear qualified for an international position, he needs to develop an international objective and then relate his international experience and patterns of achievement to that objective. Notice how we attempt to make this international linkage in the case of an individual with little international work experience.

In the second example, this same individual seeks a building inspection position in a very tight job market related to his architecture and construction skills. This is the first résumé this individual has ever written. The résumé represents a significant career change—from an independent contractor to a salaried employee. In making this career change, George Willington presents his skills as **patterns of accomplishments** related to his architectural and construction experience.

The third example could be used for either a domestic or international position. Here the objective is generic enough to be used with a variety of different employers. We've also elaborated more on the "Project Management" experience section since this is his strongest skill and it reinforces the objective.

The outcome of these three different résumés is that George Willington acquired an exciting and flexible building inspection position which could eventually lead to some international work. It also allows him to pursue several other professional and personal interests. The job represents an excellent "fit" with his on-going and evolving professional skills and personal interests. He's using the skills he most enjoys using as well as acquiring new knowledge and experience in both the architectural and construction fields.

GEORGE WILLINGTON
1131 N. Bridge Road
Baltimore, MD 21027
301/111-0000

OBJECTIVE:	An overseas construction management/supervision position with an international design/build firm.
EDUCATION:	New York Institute of Technology Albany, New York Bachelor of Architecture, 1985
	Technische Universitat Hannover, Doctoral Program Hanover, Germany World Student Fund Fellowship, 1987

AREAS OF EFFECTIVENESS

MANAGEMENT:	Owner and President for 12 years of a design/build firm with annual revenues between 1 and 2 million.
CONSTRUCTION:	Direct experience with most methodologies of construction including wood frame, masonry, and light metal.
SUPERVISION:	Responsible for 15 full-time employees. Concurrently supervised several hundred sub-contractors/crews. Many crews were non-English speaking.
ARCHITECTURAL DESIGN:	• Residential experience with custom and track family homes ranging from 1000 to 10,000 square feet. • Commercial experience with retail, office, office/warehouse, warehouse, restaurants, and marinas.
OVERSEAS:	• Fluent in German, written and spoken. • Experienced working, researching, and residing abroad—11 years in northern Europe and several Third World countries.
COMMUNITY:	President of Western Maryland Building Industries Association, an affiliate of The National Association of Home Builders.
ADDITIONAL SKILLS AND EXPERIENCE:	• Computer Proficient (including Acad) • P-IFR Pilot • U.S. Coast Guard Commercial Captains License • Ham Radio Operator • Co-author of 3 books
PERSONAL:	44, single, excellent health, enthusiastic to travel and/or relocate for the appropriate challenge.

GEORGE WILLINGTON
1131 N. Bridge Road
Baltimore, MD 21027
301/111-0000

OBJECTIVE: A building inspection position involving all phases of both residential and commercial construction.

EDUCATION: New York Institute of Technology
Albany, New York
Bachelor of Architecture, 1985

Technische Universitat Hannover, Doctoral Program
Hanover, Germany
World Student Fund Fellowship, 1987

AREAS OF EFFECTIVENESS

MANAGEMENT: Owner and President for 12 years of a design/build firm with annual revenues between 1 and 2 million.

CONSTRUCTION: Direct experience with most methodologies of construction including wood frame, masonry, and light metal.

SUPERVISION: Responsible for 15 full-time employees. Concurrently supervised several hundred sub-contractors/crews.

ARCHITECTURAL DESIGN:

- Residential experience with custom and tract family homes, ranging from 1000 to 10,000 square feet.

- Commercial experience with retail, office, office/warehouse, warehouse, restaurants, and marinas.

COMMUNITY: President of Western Maryland Building Industries Association, an affiliate of The National Association of Home Builders.

ADDITIONAL SKILLS AND EXPERIENCE:

- Computer Proficient (including Acad)
- P-IFR Pilot
- U.S. Coast Guard Commercial Captains License
- Ham Radio Operator
- Co-author of 3 books

PERSONAL: 44, excellent health, willing to travel and/or relocate for the appropriate challenge.

GEORGE WILLINGTON
1131 N. Bridge Road
Baltimore, MD 21027
301/111-0000

OBJECTIVE: A construction/contract management position on a multi-faceted project requiring strong managerial, scheduling, and supervisory skills.

EDUCATION: New York Institute of Technology
Albany, New York
Bachelor of Architecture, 1985

Technische Universitat Hannover, Doctoral Program
Hanover, Germany
World Student Fund Fellowship, 1987

AREAS OF EFFECTIVENESS

PROJECT MANAGEMENT: Owner and President for 12 years of a multi-million dollar design/build firm. Involved in all phases of project management, including contract negotiations, change order administration, scheduling, and personnel.

CONSTRUCTION: Direct experience with most methodologies of construction including wood frame, masonry, and light metal.

SUPERVISION: Responsible for 15 full-time employees. Concurrently supervised several hundred sub-contractors/crews.

ARCHITECTURAL DESIGN:
- Residential experience with custom and tract family homes, ranging from 1000 to 10,000 square feet.
- Commercial experience with retail, office, office/warehouse, warehouse, restaurants, and marinas.

OVERSEAS:
- Fluent in German, written and spoken.
- Experienced working, researching, and residing abroad—11 years in northern Europe and several Third World countries.

COMMUNITY: President of Western Maryland Building Industries Association, an affiliate of The National Association of Home Builders.

ADDITIONAL SKILLS AND EXPERIENCE:
- Computer Proficient (including Acad)
- P-IFR Pilot
- U.S. Coast Guard Commercial Captains License
- Ham Radio Operator
- Co-author of 3 books

PERSONAL: 44, excellent health, willing to travel and/or relocate for the appropriate challenge.

6

Dynamite Résumé Sampler

The résumé examples in this chapter illustrate different educational, experience, and occupational levels. Each résumé follows the principles outlined in previous chapters. All of these résumés are more or less scanable. Individuals with technical backgrounds, such as Suzanne Russell on pages 137-138, have a much richer mix of keywords than individuals who are looking for jobs as police officers (page 136) or flight attendants (page 141).

The résumés on pages 118-121 and 141 reflect different educational and experience levels. The résumé on page 118, for example, is for a high school graduate with vocational skills and experience. The résumé on page 119 is for a junior college graduate with a non-traditional background. The résumé on page 120 is appropriate for a recent B.A. graduate. The résumé on page 141 is actually from a high school graduate, but we decided to omit educational background altogether since it might be a negative for this individual. In fact, no one noticed this missing category, and she did get several interviews for flight attendant positions.

The example on pages 121-122 differs from all others. Especially appropriate for individuals with an M.A. or Ph.D. degree, or for those with specialized research, publication, and other production experience, this example includes an add-on supplemental sheet which lists relevant qualifications. The main résumé is still one page. The add-on sheet is designed to reinforce the major thrust of the résumé without

116

distracting from it. This is an ideal résumé for someone who needs to include examples of their work within the framework of the one to two-page résumé.

The remaining résumés in this chapter represent different occupations and positions such as accounting, attorney, bookkeeping, computers, construction, financial analyst, international development, paralegal, publishing, sales, police officer, telecommunications, industrial engineering, financial services, and travel. Several examples use a "Summary of Qualifications" and a two-page résumé. The résumés on pages 130-138 are appropriate for transitioning military personnel. The résumé on page 139 is for an immigrant from Ghana and the former Soviet Union who is seeking an international job.

> **Stressing skills and productivity, these are both employer-centered and value-added résumés. They clearly illustrate key résumé principles.**

While the résumés presented in this chapter are from individuals with different occupational, skill, experience, and educational backgrounds, they in no way represent résumés in general. That's not our purpose. Rather, our purpose in presenting this particular set of résumés is to clearly illustrate the major résumé writing principles outlined throughout this book. In each case, individual résumé elements relate to a carefully stated job objective. Stressing skills and productivity, these are value-added résumés; they are employer-centered rather than self-centered. Several of the examples are appropriate for career changers.

ARCHITECTURAL DRAFTER

JOHN ALBERT
1099 Seventh Avenue
Akron, OH 44522
322/645-8271

OBJECTIVE: **A position as architectural drafter** with a firm specializing in commercial construction where technical knowledge and practical experience will enhance construction design and building operations.

EXPERIENCE: <u>Draftsman</u>: Akron Construction Company, Akron, OH. Helped develop construction plans for $14 million of residential and commercial construction. (1997 to present).

<u>Cabinet Maker</u>: Jason's Linoleum and Carpet Company, Akron, OH. Designed and constructed kitchen counter tops and cabinets; installed the material in homes; cut and laid linoleum flooring in apartment complexes. (1993 to 1996).

<u>Carpenter's Assistant</u>: Kennison Associates, Akron, OH. Assisted carpenter in the reconstruction of a restaurant and in building of forms for pouring concrete. (Summer 1990).

<u>Materials Control Auditor</u>: Taylor Machine and Foundry, Akron, OH. Collected data on the amount of material being utilized daily in the operation of the foundry. Evaluated the information to determine the amount of materials being wasted. Submitted reports to production supervisor on the analysis of weekly and monthly production. (Summer 1991)

TRAINING: <u>Drafting School, Akron Vocational and Technical Center</u>, 1994. Completed 15 months of training in drafting night school.

EDUCATION: <u>Akron Community High School</u>, Akron, OH. Graduated in 1991.

PERSONAL: 28...single...willing to relocate...prefer working both indoors and outdoors...strive for perfection...hard worker...enjoy photography, landscaping, furniture design and construction.

REFERENCES: Available upon request.

SYSTEMS ANALYSIS/
MANAGEMENT INFORMATION SYSTEMS

GARY S. PLATT
2238 South Olby Road, Sacramento, CA 97342
712/564-3981
plattg@aol.com

OBJECTIVE

A position in the areas of systems analysis and implementation of Management Information Systems which will utilize a demonstrated ability to improve systems performance. Willing to relocate.

RELATED EXPERIENCE

Engineering Technician, U.S. Navy.
    Reviewed technical publications to improve operational and technical descriptions and maintenance procedures. Developed system operation training course for high-level, nontechnical managers. Developed PERT charts for scheduling 18-month overhauls. Installed and checked out digital computer equipment with engineers. Devised and implemented a planned maintenance program and schedule for computer complex to reduce equipment down-time and increase utilization by user departments. (1994 to present)

Assistant Manager/System Technician, U.S. Navy, 37 person division.
    Established and coordinated preventive/corrective maintenance system for four missile guidance systems (9 work centers) resulting in increased reliability. Advised management on system operation and utilization for maximum effectiveness. Performed system test analysis and directed corrective maintenance actions. Interfaced with other managers to coordinate interaction of equipment and personnel. Conducted maintenance and safety inspections of various types of work centers. (1990 to 1993)

Assistant Manager/System Technician, U.S. Navy, 25 person division.
    Supervised system tests, analyzed results, and directed maintenance actions on two missile guidance systems. Overhauled and adjusted within factory specifications two special purpose computers, reducing down-time over 50%. Established and coordinated system and computer training program. During this period, both systems received the "Battle Efficiency E For Excellence" award in competition with others units. (1987 to 1989)

EDUCATION

U.S. Navy Schools, 1992-1996:
    Digital System Fundamentals, Analog/Digital Digital/Analog Conversion Techniques, UNIVAC 1219B Computer Programming, and Technical Writing.

A.S. in Education, June 1990:
    San Diego Community College, San Diego, CA
    Highlight:
        Graduated Magna Cum Laude
        Member, Phi Beta Kappa Honor Society

RESEARCH/LAW ENFORCEMENT ADMINISTRATION

CHERYL AYERS
2589 Jason Drive
Ithaca, NY 14850

202/467-8735
Ayersc@aol.com

OBJECTIVE: A research, data analysis, and planning position in law enforcement administration which will use leadership, responsibility, and organizational skills for improving the efficiency of operations.

EDUCATION: **B.S. in Criminal Justice**, 1997
Ithaca College, Ithaca, NY
- Major: Law Enforcement Administration
- Minor: Management Information Systems
  G.P.A. in concentration 3.6/4.0

AREAS OF EFFECTIVENESS:

Leadership
Head secretary while working at State Police.
Served as Rush Chair and Social Chair for Chi Phi Sorority.
Elected Captain and Co-Captain three times during ten years of cheerleading.

Responsibility
Handled highly confidential information, material, and files for State Police.
Aided in the implementation of on-line banking system.
In charge of receiving and dispersing cash funds for drive-in restaurant.

Organization
Revised ticket system for investigators' reports at State Police.
Planning schedules and budget, developed party themes and skits, obtained prop material, and delegated and coordinated work of others during sorority rush.

Data Analysis
Proficient in dBase, Excel, and Access.
Analyzed State Police data on apprehensions; wrote report.

PERSONAL: 24...excellent health...single...enjoy all sports and challenges...willing to relocate.

REFERENCES: Available upon request from the Office of Career Planning and Placement, Ithaca College, Ithaca, NY

PUBLIC RELATIONS

MICHELE R. FOLGER
733 Main Street
Williamsburg, VA 23572
804/376-9932
folgerm@aol.com

OBJECTIVE:	A manager/practitioner position in public relations which will use research, writing, and program experience. Willing to relocate.

EXPERIENCE:

Program Development
Conducted research on the representation of minority students in medical colleges. Developed proposal for a major study in the field. Secured funding for $945,000 project. Coordinated and administered the program which had major effect on medical education.

Initiated and developed a national minority student recruitment program for 20 medical colleges.

Writing
Compiled and published reports in a variety of educational areas. Produced several booklets on urban problems for general distribution. Published articles in professional journals. Wrote and presented conference papers.

Research
Gathered and analyzed information concerning higher education in a variety of specialized fields. Familiar with data collection and statistics. Good knowledge of computers.

Administration and Management
Hired and trained research assistants. Managed medium-sized office and supervised 30 employees.

Public Relations
Prepared press releases and conducted press conferences. Organized and hosted receptions and social events. Spoke to various civic, business, and professional organizations.

WORK HISTORY:	ATS Research Associates, Washington, DC Virginia Education Foundation, Richmond, VA Eaton's Advertising Agency, Cincinnati, OH
EDUCATION:	M.A., Journalism, College of William and Mary, 1994. B.A., English Literature, University of Cincinnati, 1988.
REFERENCES:	Available upon request.

SUPPLEMENTAL INFORMATION   **MICHELE R. FOLGER**

Public Speaking

- "The New Public Relations," New York Public Relations Society, New York City, April 8, 1998.
- "How to Prepare an Effective Press Conference," Virginia Department of Public Relations, Richmond, Virginia, November 21, 1997.
- "New Approaches to Public Relations," United States Chamber of Commerce, Washington, D.C., February 26, 1996.

Professional Activities

- Delegate, State Writer's Conference, Roanoke, VA, 1997.
- Chair, Journalism Club, College of William and Mary, 1996.
- Secretary, Creative Writing Society, University of Cincinnati, 1995.
- Co-Chair, Public Relations in the United States Conference, College of William and Mary, 1994.
- Chair, Women's Conference, Junior League of Cincinnati, 1993.

Publications

- "The Creative Writer Today," Times Literary, Vol. 6, No. 3 (September 1997), pp. 34-51.
- "Representation of Minority Medical Students," Medical Education, Vol. 32, No. 1 (January 1996), pp. 206-218.
- "Recruiting Minority Students to Medical Colleges in the Northeast," Medical College Bulletin, Vol. 23, No. 4 (March 1995), pp. 21-29.

Reports

- "Increasing Representation of Minority Students in 50 Medical Colleges," submitted to the Foundation for Medical Education, Washington, DC, May 1997, 288 pages.
- "Urban Education as a Problem of Urban Decay," submitted to the Urban Education Foundation, New York City, September 1996, 421 pages.

Continuing Education

- "Grantsmanship Workshop," Williamsburg, Virginia, 1997.
- "Developing Public Relations Writing Skills," workshop, Washington, D.C., 1995.
- "New Program Development Approaches for the 1990's," Virginia Beach, Virginia, 1994.
- "Research Design and Data Analysis in the Humanities," University of Michigan, 1993.

Educational Highlights

- Assistant Editor of the Literary Times, University of Cincinnati, 1990-1991.
- Earned 3.8/4.0 grade point average as undergraduate and 4.0/4.0 as graduate student while working full time.
- M.A. Thesis: "Creating Writing Approaches to Public Relations."

PUBLISHING/COMPUTERS

MARY FURNISS
7812 W. 24th St.
Dallas, TX 71234

821/879-1124
furnissm@aol.com

OBJECTIVE:	**A management position** involving the application of computer technology for improving the efficiency of publishing operations.
EXPERIENCE:	<u>**Computer Applications Manager, 1995 to present**</u> Stevens Publishing Company, Fort Worth, TX Managed all computer-related projects for publishing firm with annual sales of $40 million. Presented yearly capital expenditure and general systems budget, negotiated computer service contracts, evaluated and recommended new equipment and software purchases, and trained staff to use software and hardware. Replaced ATEX typesetting with desktop publishing system that immediately saved the company $650,000 in operational costs. <u>**Editorial/Production Supervisor, 1992-1994**</u> Benton Publishing Company, San Francisco, CA Supervised all computer-related projects. Trained staff of 27 to use WordPerfect and other software applications. Devised an innovative system that transformed traditional galley editing into an efficient electronic editing system. New computerized system eliminated the need for two additional employees to handle the traditional galley editing system. Reduced errors by 70 percent. <u>**Editorial Assistant, 1990-1991**</u> Benton Publishing Company, San Francisco, CA Prepared annual *Encyclopedia of International Forestry* materials for editing and production. Supervised freelancers for special editorial projects. Proofread and copy-edited materials for 18 books produced annually. Received "Employee of the Year" award for initiating a new computerized editing system that saved the company $70,000 in annual freelance editing fees.
EDUCATION:	<u>**University of Washington**</u> B.A., Journalism, 1990.
SPECIAL SKILLS:	Familiar with the ATEX typesetting system and the application of Ventura desktop publishing software. Attended two advanced training programs in the use of computerized editing systems.
PERSONAL:	Enjoy developing innovative and cost-saving approaches to traditional publishing tasks that involve the application of computer technology. Work well in team settings and with training groups. Willing to relocate for the appropriate challenge.

CONSTRUCTION/PROJECT MANAGER

JAMES BARSTOW
7781 West Gate Road
Cincinnati, OH 44411

421/827-0841
barstowj@aol.com

OBJECTIVE

A challenging project manager position involving all phases of construction where a demonstrated record of timely and cost-effective completion of projects is important to both the company and its clients.

SUMMARY OF QUALIFICATIONS

- 28 years of progressively responsible construction management experience involving all facets of construction, from start-up to final inspection.
- Experienced in supervising all aspects of construction including masonry, concrete work, carpentry, electrical, mechanical, and plumbing.
- Communicate and work well with individuals at all levels from client to architect to subcontractors.

EXPERIENCE

Independent Contractor, Barstow & Thomas, Cincinnati, OH

Owned and managed a general contracting company doing $8 million in commercial construction each year. Performed all estimating, established contacts with subcontractors, purchased specialty items and materials, and handled shop drawings. Managed all time scheduling, monthly and submonthly draws, and guaranties. Hired all superintendents. Completed most jobs within 30 days of projected completion dates and managed to keep costs 5 percent under estimates. 1987 to 1998.

Job Superintendent, J.P. Snow, Columbus, OH

Supervised all work from start-up to final inspection as well as established all time schedules from start to finish. Handled shop drawings, lab testing, job testing, change orders, daily reports, job progress reports, payroll, and hiring. Worked with client, architect, and city, state, and federal inspectors. Responsible for all concrete and carpentry work including piers, beams, slabs, paving, walls, curbs, and walkways. Initiated an innovative scheduling system that saved the employer more than $60,000 in projected down-time. Consistently praised for taking initiative, providing exceptional leadership, and communicating well with clients, architects, and subcontactors. 1981-1986.

Subcontractor, Smith & Company, Columbus, OH

Conducted all bidding, estimating, and purchasing for more than 50 commercial masonry projects. Worked with both union and open shop help. Managed payroll for 75 employees during different project phases. Projects included hospitals, churches, schools, office buildings, and retail shops. 1977-1980.

ACCOUNTANT

JANET SOUTHERN
721 James Court
Chicago, IL 60029

401/281-9472
southernj@aol.com

OBJECTIVE:

An accounting/finance position where analytic and computer skills will be used for managing major accounts and acquiring new corporate clientele.

EXPERIENCE:

Accountant, J.S. Conners & Co., Chicago, IL
Analyzed accounting systems and installed new IBM ledger system for over 30 corporate accounts. Conducted training programs attended by more than 500 accountants with small businesses. Developed proposals, presented demonstration programs, and prepared reports for corporate clients. Increased new accounts by 42% over a four year period. 1993 to present.

Junior Accountant, Simon Electrical Co., Chicago, IL
Acquired extensive experience in all aspects of corporate accounting while assigned to the Controller's Office. Prepared detailed financial records for corporate meetings as well as performed basic accounting tasks such as journal entries, reconciling discrepancies, and checking records for accuracy and consistency. Assisted office in converting to a new computerized accounting system that eliminated the need for additional personnel and significantly improved the accuracy and responsiveness. 1989 to 1992.

Accounting Clerk, Johnson Supplies, Chicago, IL
Acquired working knowledge of basic accounting functions for a 200+ employee organization with annual revenues of $45 million. Prepared journal vouchers, posted entries, and completed standard reports. Proposed a backup accounting system that was implemented by the Senior Accountant. 1986 to 1988.

EDUCATION:

Roosevelt University, Chicago, IL
B.S., Accounting, 1985.
Highlights:
    Minor in Computer Science. Worked as a summer intern with Ballston Accounting Company. Honors graduate with a 3.7/4.0 GPA in all course work.

REFERENCES:

Available upon request.

PARALEGAL

CHARLES DAVIS
771 Anderson Street
Knoxville, TN 37921

421/789-5677
davisc@aol.com

OBJECTIVE:

A paralegal position with a firm specializing in criminal law where research and writing skills and an attention to detail will be used for completing timely assignments.

EDUCATION:

University of Illinois, Champaign, IL
B.A., Criminal Justice, 1997.
Highlights:
    Minor, English
    President, Paralegal Student Association, 1996.
    3.7/4.0 GPA

Rock Island Junior College, Rock Island, IL
A.A., English, 1995.

AREAS OF EFFECTIVENESS

LAW:

Completed 36 semester hours of criminal justice course work with special emphasis on criminal law. Served as an intern with law firm specializing in criminal law. Interviewed clients, drafted documents, conducted legal research, assisted lawyers in preparing court briefs. Participated in criminal justice forums sponsored by the Department of Criminal Justice at the University of Illinois.

RESEARCH:

Conducted research on several criminal cases as both a student and a paralegal intern. Experienced in examining court cases, interviewing lawyers and judges, and observing court proceedings. Proficient in using microfiche and computerized data bases for conducting legal research.

COMMUNICATION:

Prepared research papers, legal summaries, and memos and briefed attorneys on criminal cases relevant to assignments. Used telephone extensively for interviewing clients and conducting legal research.

WORK EXPERIENCE:

Paralegal Intern, Stanford and Rollins, Peoria, IL.
Summer Intern, 1996. Assigned to numerous research projects relevant to pending criminal cases.

Part-time employment.
Held several part-time positions while attending school full-time. These included student assistant in the Department of Criminal Justice, University of Illinois.

BOOKKEEPER

JANE BARROWS
997 Mountain Road
Denver, CO 80222

717/349-0137
barrowsj@aol.com

OBJECTIVE:

A manager or assistant manager position with an Accounting Department requiring strong supervisory and communication skills.

EXPERIENCE:

Manager, Accounts Payable, T.L. Dutton, Denver, CO.
Supervised 18 employees who routinely processed 200 invoices a day. Handled vendor inquiries and adjustments. Conducted quarterly accruals and reconciliations. Screened candidates and conducted annual performance evaluations. Reduced the number of billing errors by 30 percent and vendor inquiries by 25% within the first year. 1998 to present.

Supervisor, Accounts Payable, AAA Pest Control, Denver, CO.
Supervised 10 employees who processed nearly 140 invoices a day. Audited vendor invoices, authorized payments, and balanced daily disbursements. Introduced automated accounts receivable system for improving the efficiency and accuracy of receivables. 1995 to 1997.

Bookkeeper, Davis Nursery, Ft. Collins, CO.
Processed accounts payable and receivable, reconciled accounts, balanced daily disbursements, and managed payroll for a 20-employee organization with annual revenues of $1.8 million. 1991 to 1994.

Bookkeeper, Jamison's Lumber, Ft Collins, CO.
Assisted accountant in processing accounts payable and receivable and managing payroll for 40-employee organization with annual revenues of $3.2 million. 1987 to 1990.

EDUCATION:

Colorado Junior College, Denver, CO.
Currently taking advanced courses in accounting, computer science, and management.

Terrance Vo-Tech School, Terrance, CO.
Completed commercial courses, 1986.

REFERENCES:

Available upon request.

FINANCIAL ANALYST

SUSAN ALLEN
325 West End Street
Atlanta, GA 30019

402/378-9771
allens@aol.com

OBJECTIVE: **A financial analyst position** with a bank where
experience with investment portfolios will be used
for attracting new clientele.

EXPERIENCE: **Investment Analyst, First City Bank, Atlanta, GA.**
Managed $650 million in diverse portfolios for bank's major
clients which averaged 12 percent annual return on investment. Regularly met with clients, reviewed current invest-
ments, and presented new investment options for further
diversifying portfolios. Introduced biweekly newsletter for
communicating investment strategies with clients and bank
officers. 1994 to present.

Research Analyst, Georgia Bank, Atlanta, GA.
Conducted research, wrote reports, and briefed supervisor on
stock market trends and individual companies which affected
the bank's $1.2 billion securities portfolio. Worked closely
with Investment Analyst in developing new approaches to
communicating research findings and summary reports to
clients and bank officers. 1990 to 1993

**Research Assistant/Intern, Columbia Savings Bank,
Columbia, SC.**
Served as a Summer Intern while completing undergraduate
degree. Assigned as Research Assistant to Chief Analyst.
Followed stock market trends and conducted research on
selected investment banks. 1987 to 1988.

EDUCATION: **University of Miami, Miami, FL.**
MBA, Business Administration, 1989.
Focused course work on finance and management.
Thesis: "Successful Investment Strategies of Florida's
Ten Major Banks."

University of South Carolina, Columbia, SC.
B.S., Finance, Department of Commerce, 1987.
Summer Intern with Columbia Savings Bank.
Secretary/Treasurer of the Student Business Association.

REFERENCES: Available upon request.

SALES MANAGER

MARK ABLE
7723 Stevens Avenue
Phoenix, AZ 80023

802/461-0921
ablem@aol.com

OBJECTIVE:

A retail management position where demonstrated skills in sales and marketing and enthusiasm for innovation will be used for improving customer service and expanding department profitability.

SUMMARY OF QUALIFICATIONS:

Twelve years of progressively responsible experience in all phases of retail sales and marketing with major discount stores in culturally diverse metropolitan areas. Annually improved profitability by 15 percent and consistently rated in top 10 percent of workforce.

EXPERIENCE:

Sales Manager, K-Mart, Memphis, TN
Managed four departments with annual sales of nearly $8 million. Hired, trained, and supervised a culturally diverse workforce of 14 full-time and 6 part-time employees. Reorganized displays, developed new marketing approaches, coordinated customer feedback with buyers in upgrading quality of merchandize, and improved customer service that resulted in 25 percent increase in annual sales. Received "Outstanding" performance evaluation and "Employee of the Year" award. 1994 to present.

Assistant Buyer, Wal-Mart, Memphis, TN
Maintained inventory levels for three departments with annual sales of $5 million. Developed more competitive system of vendor relations that reduced product costs by 5 percent. Incorporated latest product and merchandizing trends into purchasing decisions. Worked closely with department managers in maintaining adequate inventory levels for best-selling items. 1990 to 1993.

Salesperson, Zayres, Knoxville, TN
Responsible for improving sales in four departments with annual sales of $3.5 million. Reorganized displays and instituted new "Ask An Expert" system for improved customer relations. Sales initiatives resulted in a 20 percent increase in annual sales. Cited for "Excellent customer relations" in annual performance evaluation. Worked part-time while completing education. 1987-1989.

EDUCATION:

University of Tennessee, Knoxville, TN
B.S., Marketing, 1987.
Earned 80 percent of educational expenses while working part-time and maintaining full course loads.

ATTORNEY

STEVEN MARSH	Home: 501/789-4321
2001 West James Ct.	Work: 501/789-5539
Seattle, WA 98322	marshs@aol.com

OBJECTIVE

A position in aviation law where proven management, organization, and supervisory skills and an exceptional record of success in investigating, adjudicating, settling, defending, and prosecuting cases will be used in settling cases to the benefit of employer and clients.

EXPERIENCE

Chief Circuit Defense Counsel, Davis Air Force Base, Ogden, UT
Personally defended all Flying Evaluation Boards (4), winning every one. Successfully defended felony trials covering offenses of drug use, distribution, assault, DUI, and perjury. Supervised, trained, and directed 22 attorneys and 17 paralegals responsible for total defense services across 16 Air Force installations located in 12 states. Included oversight of over 500 trials with every offense up to and including premeditated murder. 1994-1997

Chief, Aviation Settlement Branch, U.S. Air Force, Washington, DC
Directed the investigation, adjudication, and either settlement or litigation of all aviation, environmental, medical malpractice, and other tort claims filed against the Air Force. In 1988, this topped a $40 billion dollar exposure with the percentage of payout to claimed amount the lowest in over a decade. Supervised staff of 13 attorneys and 5 paralegals. Re-formulated U.S. Air Force policy on tort claim and litigation matters in conjunction with the Department of Justice leading to a better concept and application of paying the losers and spending time and resources to win-the-winners. 1992-1993

Chief, Tort Section, U.S. Air Force, Washington, DC
Supervised the investigation and recommended adjudication or litigation of all aviation tort claims against the Air Force, including the last of the Agent Orange cases and the KAL 007 Korean airliner shoot-down by the Soviet Union. Supervised staff of 3 attorneys and 1 paralegal. Recommended U.S. Air Force policy change on aviation tort claims that directly resulted in greater Agency latitude for meritorious claims independent of the previously required GAO Office requirements. 1991

Staff Judge Advocate, Stevens Air Force Base, Miami, FL
Advised top management of all legal issues to include the convening of Aircraft Accident Boards and Flying Evaluation Boards. Directed tort, labor, environmental, procurement, and criminal law procedures. During this period, defended two state environmental Notice of Violations successfully, and over 40 criminal cases were prosecuted without a single acquittal. Served as management's Chief Labor Resolution Negotiator securing settlements at 60 percent of the previously approved maximums. Supervised staff of 4 attorneys and 5 paralegals. 1988-1990

Assistant Staff Judge Advocate, Lowry Air Force Base, CO
Served as government prosecutor for over 35 trials with no acquittals. Served as government representative in over 20 administrative hearings with no losses. Counseled clients on rights/duties under state and federal law. 1984-1987

Area Defense Counsel, Marshall Air Force Base, Austin, TX
Defended over 300 clients in criminal trials, administrative hearings, or minor disciplinary concerns. 1983

Assistant Staff Judge Advocate, Myrtle Beach Air Force Base, SC
Investigated and adjudicated all claims arising from a major B-52 bomber aircraft accident, supervising team of paralegals. Government prosecutor for 12 trials and boards, with zero losses. 1982.

EDUCATION

J.D., Boston University College of Law, Boston, MA, 1982
B.A. (Political Science), University of North Carolina, Chapel Hill, NC, 1975

TRAINING

Armed Forces Staff College, Joint Service Program, Residence, 1992
Air War College, USAF, Seminar Program, 1991
Air Command and Staff College, USAF, Seminar Program, 1987
Squadron Officers School, USAF, Residence Program (Dist. Grad.), 1984
Officer Training School, USAF, Residence Program (Dist. Grad.), 1977

AWARDS

Stuart Reichart Award, Senior Attorney, HQ USAF, 1995
Ramirez Award, Outstanding Attorney Tactical Air Command, 1991
Outstanding Attorney, U.S. Air Forces Colorado, 1987

OTHER EXPERIENCE

U.S. Parole Board Hearing Member, USAF, 1995
Joint Services Consolidation Committee, 1991-1992
Navigator and Weapons Officer, U.S. Air Force, F-4 Phantom Aircraft, 100+ sorties,
   1979-1981
Police Officer, U.S. Air Force, 1977-1978

BAR MEMBERSHIPS

U.S. Supreme Court, 1995
U.S. Court of Appeals, 4th Circuit, 1991
U.S. Court of Military Appeals, 1985
Supreme Court of Massachusetts, 1982

FINANCIAL SERVICES

DONALD TERRENCE
1193 Daniel Road
St. Louis, MO 60000
512/888-1121 (H) / 512/888-1112 (W)
terrence@erols.com

OBJECTIVE: A financial services position where strong communication and leadership skills will result in increased sales.

ACCOMPLISHMENTS:

Financial Management Assisted in developing a $12 million annual budget for a department of 180 employees. Introduced new cost-cutting measures that resulted in saving $500,000 in a single year.

Leadership Held various leadership and staff positions (Platoon Leader, Company Commander, Executive Officer, Personnel Staff Officer) while serving in the U.S. Army. Received three commendations for quality of performance.

Communication Coordinated aviation training for the Third Armored Division, Frankfurt, Germany (17,000 soldiers, 360 armored vehicles, and 120 helicopters). Implemented a new unit training system for the division. System rated the best and most innovative in Germany.

Training Raised training ratings from the worst to the best for six helicopter attack companies on two evaluations. Received a Zero Aircraft Accident Safety Award, and raised aircraft readiness rate to 85% which was 15% above the standard.

WORK HISTORY: **Assistant Athletic Director, Administration**, U.S. Military Academy, 1993-1998.

Division Aviation Staff Officer, Third Armored Division, Germany, 1990-1992.

Aviation Company Commander, 111th Helicopter Company, Fort Rucker, AL, 1988-1989

Infantry and Aviation Officer, Fort Benning, GA, 1984-1987.

EDUCATION: **University of Michigan, Ann Arbor, MI**
M.S. in Business Administration, 1992

United States Military Academy, West Point, NY
B.S. in General Engineering, 1984

INDUSTRIAL ENGINEERING

JEFFREY THOMPSON
391 Taylor Avenue
Denver, CO 80808

Home: 499/217-3219
Work: 499/217-9123
Thompsonj@aol.com

OBJECTIVE: An industrial engineering position with a broad-based manufacturing firm.

EXPERIENCE:

Systems Analysis

- Developed mainframe-based computer forecasting models to predict an individual's risk for selection by a separation board.
- Designed computer programs that resulted in removing 2,000 erroneous records.
- Created and implemented a system acceptance testing plan for a $3 million out-sourced optimization model resulting in four critical design enhancements and an 8.2% reporting accuracy increase.

Data Automation

- Developed a PC-based pavement management decision support systems; saved $200,000 in first six months through quantitative decision analysis.
- Automated typewriter-based office environment reducing administrative processing time by 35%

Personnel Management

- Managing human resource matters for a 750 employee organization including compensation and benefits, education, legal support, performance appraisals, reassignments, and personnel strength.

Management

- Supervised 180 employees with 34 different specialty skills performing maintenance and supply operations.
- Managed a 24-hour repair and warehouse facility servicing 13 retail customers' vehicles, missile, and communications equipment valued at $2.1 million.

WORK HISTORY:

- **Operations Research and Systems Analyst**, US Total Army Personnel Command, Alexandria, VA, 1996-present.

- **Consultant**, Massachusetts Department of Public Works, Wellesley, 1994-1995.

- **Personnel Officer**, US Army, 3rd Support Command, Giessen, Germany, 1992-1993.

- **General Manager**, US Army, 32d Army Air Defense Commands, Sweinfurt, Germany, 1989-1991.

EDUCATION:

University of Massachusetts, Amherst, MA.
M.S. in Industrial Engineering and Operations Research, 1996.

Louisiana State University, Baton Rouge, LA.
B.S. in Industrial Engineering, 1987, Deans List.

PRODUCT MANAGEMENT/TELECOMMUNICATIONS

CHRIS JACKSON   Home: 413/658-9877
1922 American Way   Work: 413/658-8993
Cincinnati, OH 45556   Jacksonc@aol.com

OBJECTIVE:	A product management position in a fast growing cellular communication company where organization, leadership, and communication experience will be used for improving product quality and innovation.
EXPERIENCE:	
Organization	Designed and coordinated communications for Pacific Command Joint Training Exercises. Organized and chaired engineering conferences. Presented decision briefings and prepared staff action papers for a variety of communication-related issues of considerable importance to the command. Served as Watch Officer during operations and exercises.
Leadership	Installed, operated, and maintained satellite, switching, cable, and message communications in support of numerous U.S. Army units distributed throughout central Germany. Led 110 soldiers in performing all assigned communications missions. Total responsibility for the training, morale, welfare and discipline of all the soldiers under my command.
Communication	Planned and supervised installation of telecommunication systems of V Corps exercises. Maintained and accounted for vehicle and communications equipment valued at approximately $1.5 million. Planned and conducted individual and collective training in technical skills and general military subjects. Supervised, trained, and led 23 personnel.
WORK HISTORY:	<u>Communication Staff Officer</u>, 12th Signal Brigade, Fort Lewis, Washington, 1997-1998. <u>Communications Company Commander</u>, C Company, 430th Signal Battalion, Mainz, West Germany, 1995-1996. <u>Platoon Leader</u>, B Company, 17th Signal Battalion, Hoechst, West Germany, 1982-1984.
EDUCATION & TRAINING:	▪ U.S. Army Directory of Information Management Course, Fort Gordon, GA, 1994 ▪ B.A., Psychology, Brigham Young University, Salt Lake City, UT, 1985-1989

ORGANIZATIONAL DEVELOPMENT

CHRIS MASON
4810 Grant Circle
Louisville, KY 41016
(999) 752-4832
masonc@infinet.com

OBJECTIVE

An organizational development position with a security company requiring leadership and management expertise.

SUMMARY OF EXPERIENCE

Fourteen years of leadership and training experience. Responsible for organizing, motivating, and directing soldiers in accomplishing assigned missions.

WORK HISTORY

Platoon Sergeant, 24th Division, Fort Stewart, GA (1996-present).
Responsible for the well-being, discipline, morale, and readiness of a 30-member unit. Set and enforced high standards in the areas of personal appearance, physical fitness, and weapons qualifications. Demonstrated essential leadership, supervision, management, and team building skills for accomplishing the platoon's mission.

Training NCO, 5th Infantry Division, Fort Polk, LA (1992-1995).
Assisted in developing weekly training plans for the company. Helped establish and conduct training programs in the areas of nuclear biological and chemical protection, physical fitness, land navigation, weapons qualifications, and equipment maintenance.

Infantry Squad Leader, 3rd US Infantry, Fort Myer, VA (1988-1990).
Organized and led a 10-member team through numerous missions. Planned team work schedules and training for accomplishing mission objectives. Set and enforced high standards of performance.

Team Leader, 197th Infantry Brigade, Fort Benning, GA (1986-1987).
First line supervisor responsible for the productivity of a four-man team. Organized training, planned daily activities, and supervised team members.

EDUCATION AND TRAINING

- Infantry Advanced Noncommissioned Officers Course, 1991
- Infantry Basic Noncommissioned Officers Course, 1989
- Leadership Development Course, Noncommissioned Officers Academy, 1987
- Infantry Basic Training, 1985

POLICE OFFICER

ALLEN STRONG   Home: 139/287-2256
59 Watergate Road, Apt. 1   Work: 139/287-7667
New Orleans, LA 77777   Stronga@aol.com

OBJECTIVE

Become a police officer in a diversified, bilingual community where leadership and communication skills will be used for improving community relations.

EXPERIENCE

Training: Provided the Battalion's soldiers with training in Infantry tactics, land navigation, physical fitness, marksmanship, weaponry, leadership, and drill and ceremonies. Raised overall proficiency level from 75% to 90%.

Leadership: Served as an Infantry squad leader responsible for the discipline, morale, and training of ten soldiers. Counseled and motivated soldiers in all aspects of military training.

Weapons Proficiency: Developed proficiency in light weapon systems. Became the recognized expert in land navigation. Received award for Best Soldier of the Quarter.

WORK HISTORY

Training NCO, 75th Infantry Battalion, 82nd Airborne Division, Fort Bragg, NC, 1995-1997.

Squad Leader, 82nd Airborne Division, Fort Bragg, NC, 1994.

Infantry Scout, 82nd Airborne Division, Fort Bragg, NC, 1992-1993.

EDUCATION

- Air Assault School, 1996
- Primary Leadership Development Course, Fort Benning, GA, 1995
- Airborne School, 1993
- Basic Infantry Course, 1992
- High School Diploma, Freedom High, Tallahassee, FL, 1991

PERSONAL

Secret security clearance

TELECOMMUNICATIONS/NETWORKING

SUZANNE RUSSELL
891 Galveston Drive
Las Vegas, NV 89321

Home: (277) 975-1467   russells@aol.com   Work: (277) 975-1988

OBJECTIVE

A technical position with a dynamite telecommunication firm specializing in the design, development, and fielding of local area networks.

HIGHLIGHTS OF QUALIFICATIONS

- Five years experience with microcomputers, desktop applications, and local area networks (LANs).
- Installed cable and connected associated LAN/WAN hardware.
- Skilled in recognizing and troubleshooting problems with network and computer systems.
- Committed to patient, observant, and personable interaction with users and their problems.

RELEVANT EXPERIENCE

Network Administrator

- Loaded software for 100 terminals.
- Skilled in troubleshooting Ethernet networks.
- Added, deleted, and updated users and mail groups for a 100 terminal, 200 user 3Com Network.
- Analyzed networks using Network General's Sniffer protocol analyzer.
- Tested new software for LAN compatibility.
- Coordinated System Trouble Reports.

Software Instructor

- Trained users to be self-sufficient on a 100 terminal, 200 user LAN:
    — Introduced the Macintosh operating system;
    — Introduced the 3+Share network operating system;
    — Taught the 3+Mail E-mail program;
    — Taught the application, Microsoft Works.
- Taught advanced word processing and desktop publishing using Microsoft Word, version 4.0 for the Macintosh.
- Received an Army Achievement medal for exceptional computer training while stationed in Fort Lewis, WA.

Computer Operator

- Developed and maintained a large tape and disk library.
- Made RS-232 connectors for twisted pair cables and installed cabling.
- Installed Etherlink cards.
- Installed math co-processors in 40 PCs.
- Prepared color graphics and color slide presentations.
- Designed and edited the unit newsletter.

ADDITIONAL TECHNICAL EXPERIENCE

- Knowledge and experience with Unix and DEC VAX VMS operating systems.
- Knowledge and experience with MS-DOS and Macintosh operating systems.
- Knowledge and experience with the following IBM PC applications: MS Works, MS Word, MacDraw II, MacDraw Pro, MacPaint, SuperPaint, MS Excel, and Aldus Pagemaker.

WORK HISTORY

Served in the U.S. Army from 1994 to the present. Held positions of increasing responsibility in the areas of local area networks and microcomputer-based systems. Trained military personnel in a variety of desktop software applications. Assigned to bases in Panama and at Ft. Sill, Oklahoma and Fort Lewis, Washington. Acquired experience in the following positions:

- **Network Administrator**, Fort Stewart, GA, 1996-present
- **Instructor, Fort Lee**, VA, 1995
- **Computer Operator**, Fort Lee, VA, 1994

EDUCATION AND TRAINING

Education

- Completing a B.S. in Computer Information Systems, University of Washington, Seattle, WA.

Training

- 3Com 3+Network Installation and Administration.
- 3Com Network Architectures, Standards, and Protocols.
- Network General's Introduction to LAN Technology and Analysis.
- Network General's Ethernet Network Analysis and Troubleshooting.
- U.S. Army Ultrix/Unix Systems Operations.

INTERNATIONAL RURAL DEVELOPMENT

MARCIA TAYLOR   Home: 817/568-7311
1305 Jefferson Street   Work: 817/568-1111
Boston, MA 02311   taylorm@aol.com

OBJECTIVE

A position with an NGO specializing in rural development, where experience in proposal development, policy analysis, and project planning, monitoring, and evaluation relevant to agricultural economics and women in development in Africa and the Ukraine will be used for successful project implementation.

PROFESSIONAL EXPERIENCE

<u>Administrative Officer</u>: Collins Training Group, 9614 Lightning Road, Boston, MA 02182. Responsible for organizing administrative packages for training programs conducted by a major government contractor and private training organization. Responsibilities include scheduling and evaluating training sites, coordinating logistics, communicating with sales and instructional staff, and monitoring the implementation of contracts. 1996 to present.

<u>Planning and Monitoring Officer</u>: Department of Agricultural Extension Services, Ministry of Agriculture, Accra, Ghana. Major responsibility for planning, coordinating, and monitoring Ghana's decentralized planning process.

Planning

- Worked with 10 regions (including 118 administrative districts) in collecting and compiling plans for developing the national extension program. Assessed regional objectives. Coordinated technical, health, nutrition, and research staffs to implement the national extension program.

- Managed the review and evaluation of the Extension Services Department for organizational restructuring.

Monitoring

- Developed simplified monitoring formats to assess extension activities at all national and regional levels. Conducted periodic site visits nationwide and reported findings to Director of Extension Services. Served as liaison to Policy, Planning, Monitoring, and Evaluation Department of the Ministry of Agriculture. Evaluated transportation and communication by and among field officers. Submitted quarterly and annual reports to Director of Extension. Served as the extension counterpart to the World Bank's extension representative in monitoring activities of Pilot Farmers' Association in Sekyiama, a rural Ghanaian village.

In 1995 this model department was awarded the "Best Department Award" by the Secretary of Agriculture as well as a $40 million World Bank loan for the implementation of the national extension project. 1992 to 1995.

<u>Project Officer</u>: "31st December" Women's Movement (NGO). Served as a consultant on a grassroots nationwide NGO project designed to promote the economic self-sufficiency of rural and urban Ghanaian women. Assessed and made recommendations for enhancement, redirection, and financial support of indigenous projects designed to promote women's entrepreneurial abilities. Developed a proposal for a UNIFEM-funded ($1 million) project that provided hand-dug wells in villages in the Central Region of Ghana. Represented the organization on the Ghanaian Association of Private and Voluntary Organizations in Development (GAPVOD), Ghana's national organization of NGOs. August, 1992 to November, 1992.

Agricultural Economist: Agricultural Services Rehabilitation Project and Department of Foreign Economic Relations under the Ministry of Agriculture, Accra, Ghana. Assisted in developing proposals to international funding agencies (World Bank, FAO, USAID, IFAD) for support of agricultural programs. Undertook feasibility studies for the introduction of various agricultural projects funded by international agencies to support small-scale farmerholder projects in Northern and Volta regions. Projects analyzed agricultural potential along with the infrastructural base for project implementation (research, technology transfer, production, marketing outlets, processing, and distribution of farm produce. Study resulted in developing systems for health care, education, and agricultural cooperatives. Represented the Ministry of Agriculture at various bilateral and multilateral commission meetings. Worked with trade ministries of other African countries on negotiated trade agreements; assisted in evaluation of cost and price of agricultural products (pineapples, cocoa, and coffee) and foreign trade items (petroleum and heavy agricultural machinery).

Collective/State/Private Farm Researcher/Analyst/Participant: Ukraine and Moldavia. Studied, analyzed, and evaluated the comparative advantages and disadvantages of the collective, state, and private farm systems. Made policy recommendations for reorganizing the organizational structure of the three farm systems as well as for improving the quality and quantity of farm produce. Worked in all phases of farm operations. An on-going five-year study/project as part of a major undergraduate and graduate study program, 1986-1991.

EDUCATION

M.S. in Agricultural Economics, 1991
Odessa Agricultural Institute, Odessa, Ukraine

> Specialized in farm management and production economics. Program involved practical work, study, and organization development experience on five state, collective, and private farms over a five year period. Completed master's thesis on reducing agricultural production costs.

Advanced and Ordinary Level Certificates, General Sciences

> Mawuli School, Ho, Volta Region, Ghana, 1985
> Our Lady of Apostles Secondary School, Ho, Volta Region, Ghana, 1983

LANGUAGES

Multilingual. Completely fluent in Russian, English, and Twi—speaking, reading, and writing. Can work in all three languages.

FLIGHT ATTENDANT

MARILYN CARROLL   Home: 999-999-1782
2933 Stewart Drive   Work: 999-999-8765
Greensboro, NC 29999   Carrollm@aol.com

OBJECTIVE: A flight attendant position where demonstrated communication, organization, promotion, sales, and supervision skills will be used in promoting excellent customer service, and where enthusiasm, friendliness, judgment, maturity, humor, and dress and appearance are important to getting the job done.

AREAS OF EFFECTIVENESS:

Communications/Promotion
Coordinated press relations, developed advertising and promotional literature, and persuaded community leaders to sponsor programs and hire personnel. Maintained customer relations, promoted product line, and developed communication approaches for marketing publications worldwide. Promoted a variety of product lines, from food and clothing to stationery and gift items, at national and regional trade shows. Hosted receptions for community membership drives.

Selling
Several years experience selling clothing, food, stationery, books, computer software, educational videos, and gift items through trade shows, retail outlets, and direct-mail. Owned and operated a high quality jewelry business specializing in custom service; attained 100% customer satisfaction at all times. Especially enjoy meeting customers, demonstrating products, finalizing sales, and following-up customer relations.

Organizing
Directed a successful nine-year community fundraising program which resulted in completely discharging financial obligations. Involved in researching museum activities and selecting new historical sites. Sponsored and coordinated annual events for community leaders. Planned and implemented a successful political campaign. Organized the design and manufacture of custom-made jewelry. Developed art work for publications.

Supervising
Supervised major community projects and fundraising efforts. Hired and supervised employees involved in jewelry and publication businesses. Organized and supervised trade show activities, campaign workers, and young people.

WORK HISTORY:

Tyler Publications, Lincoln, NE, 1996-1998. Customer service representative and computer operator involved with maintaining customer relations, processing orders, accounting, and sales.

Community Savings Bank, Lincoln, NE, 1995-1996. Customer service involving opening new accounts, maintaining confidentiality, and handling deposits.

Mega Jewelry Co., Lincoln, NE, 1989-1994. Owner/operator involved in the sales and custom design of jewelry as well as day-to-day business operations.

Denver Merchandise Mart and Trade Center, Denver, CO, 1975-1978. Trade show sales representative.

7

Using Electronic Résumés and Databases in the New Job Market

Electronic résumés, optical scanners, résumé databases and service bureaus, commercial online services, and the Internet are literally transforming the way individuals identify job opportunities and write and distribute résumés. They also are changing the methods by which employers arrive at hiring decisions. More and more employers are relying on the Internet to recruit candidates. They also use new electronic methods for analyzing resumes and screening candidates.

The Electronic World of Résumés

During the past five years, new applications of computer technology to résumés has resulted in a revolution in how résumés are written, distributed, analyzed, stored, and retrieved. Primarily driven by large employers who need to better manage their human resource functions and thus recruit more efficiently, two major developments are responsible for this revolution:

1. The rise of the Internet as an important electronic meeting place for recruiting candidates, posting résumés, and networking for information, advice, and referrals.

2. The use of optical scanners and search and retrieval software for analyzing, sorting, storing, and retrieving large numbers of résumés.

The Internet has become the job seeker's and the employer's best friend. Job seekers can quickly access a tremendous amount of information on employers and job opportunities, participate in résumé databases, and transmit their résumé to employers via e-mail 24-hours a day. At the same time, employers can save thousands of dollars by recruiting on the Internet. They do this by announcing job openings on their own home pages and/or by using the services of commercial online employment sites, such as Monster Board, E.span, CareerPath, and CareerWeb, that allow them to post job vacancies and access résumés found in the site's résumé database. The perfect medium and electronic application, the Internet is literally transforming the nature of the job market. Savvy job seekers, as well as savvy employers and headhunters, frequently—but not exclusively—use the Internet for meeting their employment needs. It is the electronic "meet market" for the 21st century.

> The Internet has become the job seeker's and the employer's best friend. It is the electronic "meet market" for the 21st century.

At the same time, optical scanners and new search and retrieval software programs are increasingly responsible for linking candidates to employers. Indeed, during the next decade this technology may significantly alter the nature of the job market. It is already changing the way individuals find jobs, including how they write and distribute résumés. It's a revolution you need to learn to immediately ride since your next résumé may be transmitted via the Internet as well as initially "read" by computers before it gets passed on to be read by employers. Therefore, your résumé must first satisfy the software before it ever has the opportunity to grab the attention of employers.

Taken together, these two developments require job seekers to incorporate three major skills in their résumé writing and distribution activities:

1. Use the Internet to uncover job leads and post résumés

2. Communicate by e-mail

3. Design a résumé rich in the language of "keywords"

E-mailed, Scannable, and Web Résumés

Most résumé writing experts distinguish between three types of electronic résumés: e-mail, scannable, and Web. An **e-mailed résumé** follows certain formatting rules that enable applicants to transmit their résumé so it is readable by the recipient. Since it looks like e-mail, this is not a pretty résumé complete with eye-catching features. For example, your e-mailed résumé should be a plain-text or ASCII document; it should be stripped of any fancy formatting features, such as italics, bold, underlining, or bullets, and include 65 characteristics or fewer per line. Many e-mailed résumés also can be entered directly into résumé databases, scanned for keywords, and placed into electronic résumé tracking systems. This type of résumé can be of any type—chronological, combination, functional, or scannable/keyword—as long as it can be read as e-mail. However, since many e-mailed résumés also get entered into résumé databases and résumé tracking systems, you are well advised to write a scannable resume that is rich in keywords but formatted properly for e-mail transmission.

> ❑ **More employers rely on new electronic methods for screening candidates.**
>
> ❑ **When writing an electronic résumé, you need to select résumé language that is most responsive to optical scanners—keywords.**
>
> ❑ **Electronic networking gives renewed meaning to the "informational interview" as well as enables job seekers to broadcast their résumés to thousands of potential employers.**

A **scannable electronic résumé** requires close attention to the choice of résumé language. The search and retrieval software—whether used by employers to screen, sort, and store résumés or to search and retrieve résumés found in Internet databases—literally takes **keywords** selected by employers and matches them with similar keywords found on résumés. While a keyword is any word deemed to be important, many résumé keywords tend to be nouns that describe skills and accomplishments.

If, for example, an employer is looking for *"a human resources manager with ten years of progressive experience in developing training programs for mining engineers,"* a search for candidates meeting these specific qualifications (keywords include "human resource manager," "training," "mining engineer") may result in making matches with five résumés in the database. The employer receives either electronic or hard copies of the electronic résumés and further sorts the batch of candidates through more traditional means, such as telephone screening interviews.

A **Web résumé** also is known as an HTML resume. It appears on a Web site as a one- or two-page résumé or even as a multimedia résumé complete with sound and video. These résumés also may be linked to samples of work.

The new electronic job search and hiring systems have important implications for résumé writing. If you've written a conventional paper résumé rich in action verbs, you need to transform it into an electronic résumé rich in keywords and produced in a different format. When writing an electronic résumé, you must focus on using **proper résumé language** that would be most responsive for the search and retrieval software. This means knowing what keywords are best to include in such a résumé. Keywords often encompass the jargon of particular fields. Traditional "dress for success" elements, such as layout, type faces, emphasizing, paper texture, and color, are important at the second stage when being evaluated by the hiring official **after** the résumé has been retrieved electronically. The degree to which your résumé is "software sensitive" will largely determine how many employers will contact you. If your résumé lacks an appropriate mix of keywords, it will be passed over as irrelevant for further consideration.

Most conventional paper résumés do not conform to the strict rules of electronic résumés. We highly recommend two new books that will help you make the conversion to an electronic résumé: Joyce Lain Kennedy, *Résumés For Dummies* (IDG Books, 1998) and Peter D. Weddle, *Internet Résumés* (Impact Publications, 1998). Once you begin visiting various Internet employment sites, you'll have opportunities to put your résumé into their databases. Many of these sites, such as Career Path (*www.careerpath.com*) and E.span (*www.espan.com*), include a résumé builder or e-form for creating an electronic resume. In the meantime, you may want to visit two Web sites that can help you develop an electronic version of your résumé: *www.eresumes.com* and *www.resumail.com*.

New Résumé Initiatives

During the past few years numerous firms have gotten into the electronic résumé business. Résumé software firms, such as Restrac and Resumix, have pioneered the development of sophisticated résumé tracking systems for large corporations that need to better manage their human resource functions. Their products now include Web components for receiving e-mailed resumes that can be directly entered into a company's database. Other companies have developed online and off-line résumé databases to be accessed by employers in search of qualified candidates. Many companies use e-mail, online bulletin boards (newsgroups), commercial online services, and their own Web sites to post job vacancies, search for qualified candidates, and communicate with applicants.

Commercial résumé database firms and online employment services are new employer-employee networks which are redefining the job market. The job market is no longer confined just to the classified ads, employment firms, or executive search firms. These firms may bring together over 100,000 résumés into an electronic network which is constantly seeking to find "good fits" between the needs of employers and the keywords appearing on members' electronic résumés.

For individual job seekers, these electronic databases and online services enable them to quickly and conveniently conduct research on jobs and employers, acquire job information and advice, access employment data, post résumés online, and continuously target a job search toward numerous employers nationally as well as internationally. Many of the databases and services enable individuals to broadcast their résumés to thousands of potential employers who would not have been reached through more traditional job search or networking methods. These forms of electronic networking also give new meaning to the "information interview" which can be conducted with hundreds of individuals who participate in chat groups, use electronic bulletin boards, and communicate by e-mail.

The electronic job search revolution has evolved so fast, constantly changing its shape from day-to-day, that no one can say for certain where it is at present nor exactly where it is going over the next year or two or beyond. We do know the electronic job market shares one characteristic with the traditional job market—it's a truly chaotic arena. However, several cautionary "facts of life" put this revolution into perspective:

1. **Several résumé database firms that led this revolution in the early 1990s (kiNexus, Connexion, Career Placement Registry, Job Bank USA) have either gone out of business or transformed their operations** to be compatible with the latest electronic trends— the use of the Internet. A highly competitive arena for high-tech entrepreneurs in search of content, electronic employment services have not been profitable operations for most companies venturing into this arena; most must resign themselves with the expectation that this will be a long-term investment with a few "winners" emerging in perhaps five or ten years from now, and most of these winners probably will be operating as a combination for-free and for-fee employment sites on the Internet. Indeed, no one has figured out how to make much money operating these databases and services, beyond

charging employers for listing job vacancies and conducting candidate searches—traditional advertising and recruitment functions that used to be monopolized by newspapers and employment firms; individual job seekers, who expect to get employment information and enter their résumés into Internet employment sites for free, have not proved to be lucrative customers. And these two ostensible profit centers (résumé databases and services) may be in the process of disappearing altogether as more and more employers and job seekers use a combination of free and for-fee access of the Internet for electronic networking and services. Thus, we expect more and more electronic database and employment firms to emerge as well as go out of business within the next few years as the Internet continues to expand as a major information, networking, and recruitment arena for both employers and job seekers. Except for those that perform highly specialized recruitment functions, we do not expect many for-profit employment database and service firms to survive into the 21st century. The continuing fall-out of such services and firms looks inevitable in what appears to be continuing chaos in cyberspace.

2. **Most of what you may have read about the electronic job search revolution six months ago is probably obsolete by now** because of the rapid changes taking place in this employment arena. Even what we say here in this chapter on electronic networking and résumé databases will probably be obsolete within the next few months. But one thing is certain: you are best off learning to use the Internet and e-mail for electronic networking—electronic skills that will serve you well as the job market continues to evolve more and more on the Internet.

3. **The effectiveness of new electronic networking and electronic résumé databases over conventional networking and résumé distribution methods has yet to be proven nor are they necessarily in competition with each other.** The hype and hoopla about electronic networking and résumé databases is based on a vision or promise rather than on concrete performance. As with any self-proclaimed revolution, there is a tendency to get seduced by a vision of the future, lose perspective, and thus confuse promises with performance as well as the medium with the message. It's true that more and more employers and headhunters use the Internet to recruit

candidates. In fact, many savvy employers and headhunters have become committed users of the Internet because of their positive experiences in recruiting on the Internet and in saving or making money. Employers can save thousands of dollars in recruitment costs by using relatively inexpensive online employment sites (from free to $300), and many report the overall quality of candidates recruited on the Internet is better than those found through traditional classified ads in newspapers and trade journals. Savvy headhunters especially love the Internet because they can recruit many more candidates to present to their clients who have yet to incorporate the Internet into their recruiting efforts. Consequently, a headhunter may spend $150 recruiting a candidate on the Internet but then "flip" this candidate to a not-so-Internet-savvy employer for a fee of $20,000-$30,000 (standard fee structure being 20-30 percent of a candidate's first year salary). No wonder headhunters love the Internet. It's a marriage made in heaven —as long as their clients don't acquire direct Internet recruitment

> **Headhunters especially love the Internet. They may spend $150 recruiting a candidate on the Internet but then "flip" this candidate to a not-so-Internet-savvy employer for a fee of $20,000-$30,000!**

skills too soon! For an excellent overview of how the Internet works for both employers and headhunters, see Ray Schreyer and John McCarter, *The Employer's Guide to Recruiting On the Internet* (Impact Publications, 1998).

The benefits for job seekers, however, may be less apparent. The old adage that *"you get what you pay for"* probably has a lot to do with the mixed results; job seekers pay nothing to use most Internet employment sites and the results are that few ever get "hits" from employers. Since many satisfied employers and headhunters do regularly recruit on the Internet, some job seekers do indeed find jobs on the Internet—but no one knows to what extent they do. One suspects the numbers may be low for job seekers, and for good reasons. First, there are lot more individuals looking for jobs on the Internet then there are jobs available that match the skills and experience of such job seekers. Second, many job seekers using the Internet are young and experienced entry-level candidates for whom there are few jobs available; employers and headhunters using the Internet tend to look for specific skills and experience. Third, so far the technology has been primarily applied to the least effective job search activity—broadcasting résumés to employers. This has always been the least productive job search activity anyone can engage in. The evidence of performance for job seekers is largely anecdotal and most of it points in one direction—the electronic job market is most effective for employers, headhunters, and job seekers in high-demand high-tech fields or those seeking individuals with an exotic combination of skills and experience. Ironically, the anecdotal evidence tends to reinforce what we've known all along about job listings or the advertised job market—aside from the newness of the technology, there is nothing magical nor new about this revolution in reference to job search and recruitment functions. This new electronic revolution operates similarly to classified ads and executive search firms—it lists jobs and recruits for high-demand positions. Its real advantage is that it does it faster and thus saves both employers and job seekers time and money. The result may be that less than 10 percent of all jobs will be represented through the electronic databases and online services. There is little evidence that electronic networking and résumé databases are very effective for individuals seeking entry-level positions outside the current high-demand high-tech fields. However, this situation is changing as more and more individuals outside high-tech fields are including their résumés in these online databases. A great transformation is definitely underway.

4. **There's a tendency to confuse the medium with the message.**
   While fascinating to observe, there's no new magic here for getting a job through these electronic systems. The job search message remains the same: how to best develop job leads and communicate your qualifications to potential employers. An effective job search accomplishes this by connecting with jobs that best "fit" the interests and skills of the job seeker. In the past, the main mediums for doing this have been the mail, telephone, fax, and face-to-face meetings. The new electronic revolution now allows individuals to use computers and online services to quickly acquire job information, identify potential employers, and communicate qualifications to

employers by electronic means. It's like having a typewriter connected to a telephone with the capacity to interactively communicate with a vast audience. So far there is little evidence that the new medium will substantially alter the traditional job search message—communication between employer and job seeker.

5. **Despite the hype, there's no question about it—the electronic job search is here to stay and in a very big way.** More and more employers will list their vacancies online and use specialized electronic recruitment services. The main casualties of this electronic revolution will probably be (1) newspapers whose classified ad sections will continue to decline in both size and revenue as more and more of their print business goes online; (2) employment firms and career counselors who do not adapt to the new technology; and (3) several employment database firms and services that failed to move to the Internet as well as failed to solve the issue of profitability on the Internet. The main beneficiaries will be employers, headhunters, and job seekers who should be able to substantially cut their time and costs in navigating an increasingly competitive and chaotic job market. Our advice to job seekers is to learn how to incorporate this electronic component into your overall job search. A good starting point is Pam Dixon's *Job Searching Online For Dummies* (Foster City, CA: IDG Books, 1998). Learn how to use both the Internet and e-mail as you develop your repertoire of electronic job search skills. You'll need to use such skills for the 21st century!

Where Is the Revolution?

What exactly is this electronic revolution in relation to the job search? During the past five years, it has taken on several forms. One of its most basic and popular forms involves linking job seekers with employers through an electronic résumé database which may operate online (Internet) or off-line. However, given the convenience of the Internet, most résumé databases now operate online. Job seekers develop a paper or electronic version of their résumé which is either scanned into a computerized database or entered electronically via e-mail or an electronic template (e-form). In its optimal form, the electronic résumé is designed with **keywords** in mind. For a per search and/or weekly, monthly, or yearly membership fee, employers request these firms to identify a specific number of candidates who meet their vacancy requirements. Alternatively, employers may be given a password so they can directly access the database. The requirements, in the form of keywords, are input into the résumé database.

Depending on both the size of the database and the requirements of the employer, this electronic search procedure may generate anywhere from none to hundreds of résumés of potentially qualified candidates. The résumés are then sent to employers who, in turn, review them and select the best ones for initial computer or telephone screening interviews which may eventually turn into a series of job interviews and the selection of one candidate. If the employer has direct access to the résumé database, which is the case for most Internet employment sites, the employer can view the resumes online, print copies for review, and directly contact the candidate by e-mail. For the employer, this process is very quick and relatively seamless—enter a password to access the database; identify a combination of desired keywords that profile the perfect candidate, view the results of the résumé search that matches the keywords; and contact the candidate for more information or an interview.

> **Online career services enable job seekers to conduct research, join discussion groups, attend workshops, review job listings, and send résumés to employers.**

The beauty of this electronic job search system is its speed, cost, and possible effectiveness for both employers and job seekers. While employers may normally spend $1,000 to $20,000, as well as one to three months recruiting an employee, they may accomplish the same goal within one to two weeks at the cost of $100 to $300 by using the services of an electronic résumé database. While job seekers must learn to write a new type of résumé—an electronic résumé peppered with keywords that are most responsive to keyword searches—the results may be extremely worthwhile and may well revolutionize the whole concept of job seeking. Whether or not they are actively seeking employment, you may want to enter your résumé into several of these databases. Most are free to job seekers, especially the ones found on the Internet. You will be contacted by an employer if and when your résumé "matches" the employer's search criteria.

Job seekers who use the Internet in their job search can conduct research on jobs and employers, join discussion groups, attend workshops, acquire information and advice from career counselors and fellow job seekers, review thousands of job listings, and transmit résumés to employers. Traditional networking activities, which normally are done over the telephone or in face-to-face meetings, can be conducted through e-mail with hundreds of individuals who volunteer information and advice. Whether or not this is the same quality information and advice acquired through more traditional targeted networking activities is another story altogether. Nonetheless, it is another medium through which you can network for information, advice, and referrals.

Job Hunting That Never Stops

The revolutionary aspects of this new technology may eventually go far beyond just the electronic matching process that quickly links employers with job seekers. Given the "membership" nature of some electronic databases, they may revolutionize the way individuals make career moves. The notion that an individual stops job hunting after finding a job will likely be replaced with this concept of job hunting: you are always in the job market seeking opportunities. By paying an annual fee and regularly updating your résumé for the database, your résumé is always working the job market even though ostensibly you are not job hunting. You, in effect, are networking 24 hours a day, 7 days a week, 365 days a year.

The electronic job search may alter the way people think about the job hunting process. You no longer just turn it on or off when you are in need of another job. It's always turned on. Anytime of the day you can literally surf the Internet for potential job

> These new electronic job search services enable you to network 24 hours a day, 7 days a week, and 365 days a year from your home or office.

openings. On the other hand, while you may be perfectly content with your current job, as a member of XYZ Job Bank or if you've entered your résumé on an Internet employment site, you regularly hear from employers who are interested in your qualifications. You examine the competition and assess whether or not this is the time for you to make another career move. For you and thousands of other members of XYZ Job Bank, you are always prepared to make strategic job and career moves because you are literally wired so you can electronically network 24 hours a day. Unemployment, job dissatisfaction, and unexpected career shocks are not part of your career perspective or experience. Your continuous career health requires you to always be in the job market by way of your membership in XYZ Job Bank. In fact, you are likely to become a lifetime member of this organization. Over a 40-year worklife period, you may have found 10 of your employers through your membership in XYZ Job Bank. At the cost of $50 a year, this electronic job service was well worth the expense. Best of all, it reduced the anxiety of having to look for employment under adverse circumstances and through traditional job search methods that were extremely inefficient and ineffective.

Join a résumé database, or regularly put your résumé online, and your job search will never end!

Who Are the New Revolutionaries?

During the past few years numerous firms have gotten into the electronic résumé and employment businesses. Many of them use electronic e-mail, online bulletin boards, and existing commercial online computer services such as America Online, CompuServe, and Microsoft Network. Others are accessed solely through the Internet via the World Wide Web. Primarily funded by large Fortune 1,000 corporations or advertising firms, membership in the electronic employment database companies includes individuals, professional associations, and alumni, retirement, military and other groups who are interested in linking electronic résumés to member companies. These electronic résumé services have become new employer-employee networks which are redefining certain segments of the job market. The marketplace is no longer confined to the classified ads, employment firms, or executive search firms. The marketplace includes computerized databases developed by electronic résumé firms. These firms may bring together over 100,000 members into an electronic network which is constantly seeking to find "good fits" between the needs of employers and the keywords appearing on members' electronic résumés.

One of the major advantages of participating in these electronic networks is that you may have access to numerous positions that are not advertised outside the network. When a vacancy occurs or new position is created, participating employers may first turn to the network for qualified candidates before advertising the position outside the electronic network. It may be to your advantage to participate in such a network because you will have access to numerous positions and employers you might not otherwise reach through other networking means.

Résumé Databases

Résumé databases are the most passive job search activities you can engage in. All you need to do is contact a database firm or an Internet employment site which operates a résumé database, submit a résumé or complete a candidate profile form, and perhaps pay a monthly or yearly membership fee (some are free because employers pay the tariffs). The firm inputs your résumé or personal profile information in the computer along with thousands of other résumés. Employers either have online access to the database or they have the firm conduct candidate searches by screening résumés on specific position criteria. Employers often pay yearly membership fees or per search fees in order to use these databases. All the individual job seeker needs to do is submit a résumé or complete a profile form and in some cases pay a fee. Since the résumé database firm manages the electronic networking process, all the job seeker needs to do is join the network, similar to joining other types of subscription-based organizations. The job seeker then waits to see what will transpire as the computer attempts to match individual résumés with employer needs. These new résumé database systems are high-tech versions of the old résumé broadcast method.

These are very volatile businesses still attempting to resolve the issue of profitability, especially in the face of increased competition and the role of the Internet which has quickly become the major medium for electronic networking. Indeed, several major companies that pioneered such databases have gone out of business during the past few years and more are likely to do so soon.

Some of the most popular electronic résumé database firms include:

❑ **Career Net Graduate:** INET. 643 W. Crosstown Parkway, Kalamazoo, MI 49008, Tel. 616-344-3017. Designed for college students and recent graduates, this service makes résumés available to thousands of employers. This is now a free service to job seekers. You can enter your career profile online at *www.careernet.com*

❑ **Cors:**   One Pierce Place, Suite 300 East, Itasca, IL 60143, Tel. 800-323-1352, 708-250-8677 or Fax 708-250-7362. Claims to have 2.5 million résumés in its database. Contracts with employers to recruit candidates from database. Charges one-time $25 fee for entering résumé in database. Allows unlimited updates. Can complete an online form and submit it by e-mail by visiting their Web site: *www.cors.com/corspro.htm*

❑ **Electronic Job Matching:** Human Resource Management Center, 1915 N. Dale Mabry Highway, Suite 307, Tampa, FL 33607, Tel. 813-879-4100 or Fax 813-870-1883. Includes applicant résumés in database that can be accessed by employers who pay search fees. Free of charge for job seekers. Represents many different occupational fields and several experience levels. Web site: *www.hrmc.com*

❑ **Résumé-Link:** 5995 Wilcox Place, Dublin, OH 43016. Tel. 614-923-0600 or Fax 614-923-0610. Specializes in the computer and engineering fields. Includes thousands of résumés in its database. Free to job seekers who belong to a relevant professional society ($50 a year for nonmembers). Employers pay. Web site: *www.resume-link.com*

❑ **SkillSearch:** 3354 Perimeter Hill Drive, Suite 235, Nashville, TN 37211-4129, Tel. 615-834-9448 or Fax 615-834-9453. Sponsored by 100 university alumni associations, alumni associated with each sponsoring university can have their résumés included in the database for $49 a year. The SkillSearch database includes nearly 35,000 resumes. Employers pay a per-search fee to use the database. Web site: *www.skillsearch.com*

❑ **University ProNet:** 2445 Faber Place, Suite 200, Palo Alto, CA 94303-3394, Tel. 650-845-4000 or Fax 650-845-4019. Participation restricted to alumni of 20 member universities: California Institute of Technology, Carnegie-Mellon University, Columbia University, Cornell University, Duke University, Georgia Tech, Massachusetts Institute of Technology, Ohio State University, Purdue University, Stanford University, University of California at Berkeley, University of California at Los Angeles, University of Chicago, University of Illinois, University of Michigan, University of Pennsylvania, University of Texas at Austin, University of Wisconsin, U.S. Naval Academy, and Yale University. Employers, which consists of 300 corporate subscribers, pay an annual subscription fee to participate in the database. Alumni charged a one-time $35 registration fee. Operated by the alumni associations at each participating university. Can register online by going to the University ProNet Web site which links to each member university: *www.universitypronet.com*

The Internet's World Wide Web

Within the past three years, hundreds of new career-related services have appeared on the Internet's World Wide Web, and several of those which used to be accessed only through the commercial online services, such as AOL, are now available on the World Wide Web. In fact, this is where most online career networking is taking place these days.

The following organizations now operate databases and career services on the Internet's World Wide Web. Most of them offer a combination of free and fee-based services and products. Some primarily operate as job listing bulletin boards (BBS) or newsgroups:

❏ **America's Job Bank:** *www.ajb.dni.us.* Here's the ultimate "public job bank" that could eventually put some private online entrepreneurs out of business. Operated by the U.S. Department of Labor, this is the closest thing to a comprehensive nationwide computerized job bank. Linked to state employment offices, which daily post thousands of new job listings filed by employers with their offices, individuals should soon be able to explore more than a million job vacancies in both the public and private sectors at any time through this service. Since this is your government at work, this service is free. While the jobs listing cover everything from entry-level to professional and managerial positions, expect to find a disproportionate number of jobs requiring less than a college education listed in this job bank. This service is also available at state employment offices as well as at other locations (look for touch screen kiosks in shopping centers and other public places) which are set up for public use. Useful linkages.

❏ **CareerBuilder:** *www.careerbuilder.com.* A real up and coming site which uses a different approach—heavily advertises on radio, especially early in morning when individuals are commuting to work. Gets lots of hits during the noon hours when employees search their site for job listings! Employers list job vacancies in anticipation of getting hits from job seekers. Also, job seekers complete a questionnaire and receive e-mail messages when a position fits their keywords. Does not operate a résumé database since they contact you.

❏ **CareerCity:** *www.careercity.com.* Operated by one of the major publishers of career books, this online service includes job listings, discussion forums (conferences, workshops, Q&A sessions), specialized career services, and publications.

❏ **Career Magazine:** *www.careermag.com.* A very user-friendly and useful site with lots of advice, newsgroups, and links. Includes a directory of executive recruiters. Includes a résumé database.

❏ **CareerMosiac:** *www.careermosiac.com.* This job service is appropriate for college students and professionals. Includes hundreds of job listings in a large variety of fields, from high-tech to retail, with useful information on each employer and job. Includes a useful feature whereby college students can communicate directly with employers (e-mail) for information and advice—a good opportunity to do "inside" networking.

❏ **CareerPath:** *www.careerpath.com.* Over 30 major newspapers across the country participate in this site which primarily consists of newspaper classified ads being put online. Includes lots of advice as well as Richard Nelson Bolles' *What Color Is Your Parachute?* site which serves as a gateway site to many other Internet employment sites.

❑ **CareerWeb:** *www.careerweb.com.* Operated by Landmark Communications (Norfolk, Virginia) which also publishes several newspapers and operates The Weather Channel, The Travel Channel, and InfiNet, this relatively new service is a major recruitment source for hundreds of companies nationwide. Free service for job seekers who can explore hundreds of job listings, many of which are in high-tech fields. Includes company profile pages to learn about a specific company. A quality operation.

❑ **E.span:** *www.espan.com.* This full-service online employment resource includes hundreds of job listings in a variety of fields as well as operates a huge database of résumés. Job seekers can send their résumés (e-mail or snail mail) to be included in their database of job listings and search for appropriate job openings through the Interactive Employment Network. Also includes useful career information and resources.

❑ **JobTrak:** *www.jobtrak.com.* This organization posts over 500 new job openings each day from companies seeking college students and graduates. Includes company profiles, job hunting tips, and employment information. Good source for entry-level positions, including both full-time and part-time positions, and for researching companies. Very popular with college students.

❑ **JobWeb:** *www.jobweb.org.* A comprehensive online service targeted for the college scene. Operated by the National Association of Colleges and Universities (formerly the College Placement Council), this service is designed to do everything: compiles information on employers, including salary surveys; lists job openings; provides job search assistance; and maintains a résumé database.

❑ **Monster Board:** *www.monster.com.* One of the Internet's largest and most popular sites. Lots of job listings and company profiles. Owned by TMP, an advertising recruitment firm, which also owns the Online Career Center.

❑ **Online Career Center:** *www.occ.com/occ.* This is the grandaddy of career centers on the Internet. It's basically a résumé database and job search service. Individuals send their résumé (free if transmitted electronically) which is then included in the database. Individuals also can search for appropriate job openings. Employers pay for using the service. Also available through online commercial services.

Many other Web sites also have résumé databases. At the very minimum, you also should visit these sites:

4Work.com	*www.4work.com*
America's Employers	*www.americasemployers.com*
Best Jobs U.S.A.	*www.bestjobsusa.com*
Black Collegian	*www.black-collegian.com*

CareerCast	*www.careercast.com*
Career.com	*www.career.com*
CareerMart	*www.careermart.com*
CareerSite	*www.careersite.com*
Careers.wsj.com	*www.careers.wsj.com*
College Central	*www.collegecentral.com*
College Grad Job Hunter	*www.collegegrad.com*
Headhunter.net	*www.headhunter.net*
Internet Job Locator	*www.joblocator.com/jobs/*
JobBank USA	*www.jobbankusa.com*
JobDirect	*www.jobdirect.com*
NationJob Network	*www.nationjob.com*
TOPjobs USA	*www.topjobsusa.com*
Town Online Working	*www.townonline.com/working*
Westech Virtual Job Fair	*www.vjf.com*
World.Hire ONLINE	*www.world.hire.com*
Yahoo! Classifieds	*classifieds.yahoo.com/employment.html*

If you are with the military, or you are a veteran, you may want to get your résumé in the résumé databases of these excellent sites:

Green to Gray Online	*www.greentogray.com*
Blue to Gray Online	*www.bluetogray.com*
Transition Assistance Online	*www.taonline.com*

If you want to send your résumé to executive recruiters or headhunters, try these two sites:

DICE	*www.dice.com*
Recruiters Online Network	*www.ipa.com*

If you want to electronically broadcast your résumé to hundreds of companies, try these sites. All are free except for CareerSearch which charges a fee:

CareerSearch	*www.careersearch.net*
CompaniesOnline	*www.companiesonline.com*
E.span	*www.espan.com*
Resumail	*www.resumail.com*
ResumePath	*www.resumepath*

Hundreds of other Web sites, many of which are occupationally specialized, also operate résumé databases. And don't forget to contact your professional association. More and more professional associations are developing their own online services and résumé databases to better serve the career needs of their members. You may find these Web sites more useful since they are targeted toward your profession and primarily involve employers who are looking for your occupational specialty.

Other Electronic Networks

Commercial online services and career-related World Wide Web sites on the Internet are only the tip of the iceberg when it comes to electronic networking. Numerous professional groups, from the military to health care professionals, have established, or are in the process of creating, their own World Wide Web sites and bulletin boards (BBS). Most of these groups operate discussion forums and networking groups as well as post job openings. If you are just getting started with electronic networking, the groups we've identified thus far should suffice in pointing you in the right direction. Starting with these resources, you should be able to

> Learn how to network online via the Internet. Put together an electronic résumé and transmit it by e-mail.

quickly find useful linkages to other more specialized sites relating to employment issues. If you want to quickly connect to newsgroups, go to the Yahoo site which includes newsgroups under "jobs wanted" and "requests for employment": *www.yahoo.com*

If you know how to use e-mail and surf the Internet, a whole new job search world will unfold before your computer screen. You will discover new ways to network your way to job and career success. Indeed, as we write this material, several hundred new networking groups are in the process of developing sites on the Internet. Within the next 12 months many new employment players will be up and running online. Our best advice is this: you should learn how to operate online so you can discover as well as create your own electronic networking opportunities in the future. Learn how to put together an electronic résumé as well as how to transmit your résumé via e-mail. Your major challenge will be to sort through the chaos of this new electronic world to get meaningful results! This will not be as easy a task as it may initially appear.

Expect to do a lot of electronic communicating that has little or no payoff for your job search.

Key Electronic Job Search Resources

Several books provide useful information on the new electronic job search era. Among some of the most useful such resources are:

Criscito, Pat, *Résumés in Cyberspace* (Hauppauge, NY: Barrons, 1997)

Crispin, Gerry and Mark Mehler, *CareerXroads 1998* (Kendall Park, NJ: MMC Group, 1998)

Dixon, Pam, *Job Searching Online For Dummies* (Foster City, CA: IDG Books, 1998)

Glossbrenner, Alfred and Emily, *Finding a Job on the Internet* (New York: McGraw-Hill, 1995)

Gonyea, James C., *Electronic Résumés: Putting Your Résumé On-Line* (New York: McGraw-Hill, 1996)

Gonyea, James C., *The On-Line Job Search Companion* (New York: McGraw-Hill, 1995)

Jandt, Fred E. and Mary Nemnick, *Using the Internet and the World Wide Web in Your Job Search* (Indianapolis, IN: JIST Works, 1997)

Karl, Shannon and Arthur Karl, *How to Get Your Dream Job Using the Web* (Scottsdale, AZ: Coriolis Group Books, 1997)

Kennedy, Joyce Lain, *Hook Up, Get Hired* (New York: Wiley & Sons, Inc., 1995)

Kennedy, Joyce Lain, *Résumés For Dummies* (Foster City, CA: IDG Books, 1998)

Kennedy, Joyce Lain and Thomas J. Morrow, *Electronic Job Search Revolution* (New York: Wiley & Sons, Inc., 1996)

Kennedy, Joyce Lain and Thomas J. Morrow, *Electronic Résumé Revolution* (New York: Wiley & Sons, Inc. 1996)

Oakes, Elizabeth H., *Career Exploration On the Internet* (Chicago, IL: Ferguson Publishing, 1998)

Riley, Margaret, Frances Roehm, and Steve Oserman, *The Guide to Internet Job Searching* (Lincolnwood, IL: NTC Publishing, 1998)

Weddle, Peter D., *Internet Résumés* (Manassas Park, VA: Impact Publications, 1998)

Beware of the Lazy Way to Job Search Success

While electronic job search services may well be the wave of the future, especially for large and medium-sized employers, they will by no means displace the more traditional job search and résumé distribution methods identified in this book for finding jobs. These are proven methods used by thousands of successful job seekers. Indeed, there is a danger in thinking that the electronic revolution will offer **the** solution to the inefficiencies and ineffectiveness associated with traditional job search methods. As presently practiced, electronic networking is primarily a high-tech method for disseminating résumés to potential employers and for acquiring information on employers.

The problems with present forms of electronic networking are fourfold. First, most networks are primarily designed for and controlled by employers. Job seekers are only included in the networks for the benefit of employers. Indeed, these electronic networks are mostly funded by employers who have online access to participants' résumé data. Job seekers' involvement in these networks is that of passive participant who submits an electronic résumé and then waits to hear from employers who may or may not refer to their résumé. Not surprising, many job seekers may never hear from employers. From the perspective of the job seeker, such a network is merely a high-tech version of the broadcast résumé that is mass mailed to numerous employers—one of the most ineffective résumé distribution approaches. However, when it focuses on acquiring information, advice, and referrals, electronic networking may become more useful and effective for job seekers.

Second, electronic résumé services give employers limited, albeit important, information on candidates. These services are primarily efficient résumé screening techniques that communicate little information about the individual beyond traditional résumé categories. Employers still need to screen candidates on other criteria, especially in face-to-face settings, which enable them to assess a candidate's personal chemistry. Such information is best communicated by networking with your résumé.

Third, the major sponsors and participants—large to medium-sized corporations—in the electronic résumé databases are not the ones that do most of the hiring. These are the same companies that have been shedding jobs—nearly 5 million in the past eight years—rather than adding them to the job market. The companies that do the most hiring and thus add the most jobs to the workforce —small companies with fewer than 100 employees—are not major participants in the electronic job market. If you neglect these nonparticipants, you may be overlooking many job opportunities.

Fourth, the quality of information, advice, and referrals gained from electronic networking may be very poor or nearly useless because of the types of individuals participating in such relatively anonymous networks. You may, for example, be communicating with a kid, someone who is unemployed, people with little or no experience, or even a scam artist or a sociopath! Busy employers and employment experts—those who can really make a difference when you are engaged in quality networking—don't have the luxury of spending time online networking with strangers.

Create a Dynamite Résumé For All Seasons

So where does this all lead in terms of your résumé and job search? We recommend that you include electronic elements in your overall repertoire of job search methods. But put these electronic elements in their proper perspective—an efficient way to broadcast your qualifications to employers through an electronic résumé as well as acquire potentially useful information about jobs, employers, and job search methods. Don't approach electronic networking as the easy way to job search success; there's nothing magical about disseminating résumés electronically nor communicating with strangers by e-mail. Concentrate instead on developing a dynamite résumé that is most responsive to **both** optical scanners and human beings!

8

Résumé Resource Round-Up

Today's marketplace is literally flooded with résumé books as well as computer software, CD-ROMs, and videos designed to help individuals write better résumés. Indeed, résumé books tend to be the first book of choice for most people conducting a job search.

Any market with a high demand will generate numerous suppliers providing products to satisfy the demand. And like many markets, the résumé writing market exhibits many resources of questionable value.

In this chapter we examine several of these resources with an eye toward the best quality. In Chapter 7 we included information on the major electronic résumé database firms which are revolutionizing the way employers screen candidates. Many of these firms also provide resources for writing résumés. For your convenience, you can order many of these products identified in this chapter directly from Impact Publications by completing the order form at the end of this book.

Questionable Advice, Embarrassing Examples

During the past fifteen years we have had an opportunity to review many of these resources. Sad to say, it's a disappointing lot. While numerous résumé books are available, few get high marks for being particularly useful. Indeed, nearly 80 percent of the résumé books we've encountered get poor marks. Despite authors' claims to being "professional headhunters," "job search specialists," "professional résumé writers," "experienced executives who read or screen hundreds or thousands of résumés each year," or keepers of a unique set of résumés that "really did get jobs," we've not been overly impressed. Most writers tend to be unfamiliar with the major career planning and job search literature, perhaps reading only one or two relevant books. Claiming "experience" as their basis for credibility, many are unfamiliar with mainstream career planning and job search methods which are not incorporated in their books. More often than not, they give standard to poor advice and offer what might be best termed embarrassing examples. Indeed, we are surprised to find so many of these "experts" still presenting traditional chronological résumés—complete with height, weight, marital status, sex, age, dates of employment first, duties and responsibilities, and the word "Résumé" firmly planted at the top as examples of résumé excellence!

Most résumé example books tend to be compilations of résumés the authors happened to have on hand rather than examples based upon sound principles of effective résumé writing. Many are very disorganized—jumping from one unrelated topic to another. Most lack a clear approach, focus, or central organizing principle; are outdated; and are anything but user-friendly. Many arbitrarily include examples of résumés for individuals associated with 50 to 100 occupations, as if such examples were representative of over 13,000 occupations available! Furthermore, many résumé books are preoccupied with the writing exercise to the exclusion of critical how-to processes such as résumé production, distribution, follow-up, and evaluation. Few clearly link résumés to the larger job search processes of self-assessment, research, networking, and interviewing.

Even many of the latest résumé books remain obviously dated and of questionable usefulness. Above all, they neglect to address the important issue of electronic résumés—résumés specifically designed to be "read" and sorted by optical scanners—as well as fail to acquaint readers with new channels for résumé distribution, such as electronic résumé databases.

On the other hand, some new books on electronic résumés do what often happens when new technology is introduced to a field—confuse technological adaptation with process and content. Not surprising, preoccupied with the bells and whistles of computer hardware and software and demonstrating a lot of fuzzy thinking, many such books tend to overstate the role of electronic résumés in the job search for both employers and candidates. Confusing the medium with the message, they equate the notion of "keywords" (anything a computer is instructed to search for—"garbage in, garbage out") with the concept of "skills" (specific abilities transformed into accomplishments). They further confuse computer sorting functions (optical scanning) with human evaluation activities. Worst of all, they fail to demonstrate a clear understanding of the difference among résumé writing, screening, and distribution activities as well as how electronic and interpersonal networking relate to the résumé writing and distribution processes.

The result of such confused thinking is an interesting new résumé writing dilemma—electronic résumé writing advice may result in excellent "machine readable" résumés; but when distributed outside electronic mediums—where they are actually read and evaluated by employers—these same résumés may be weak products in comparison to other types of résumés. Humans **read** résumés for both form and content rather than just **scan** résumés for keywords. Therefore, your résumé should be carefully structured to satisfy both types of readers—optical scanners and employers. You must pay particular attention to **both** form and content in order to satisfy both types of "readers."

> ❑ **Few résumé example books include examples based upon sound principles of effective résumé writing.**
>
> ❑ **Only a handful of books address the critical issues of résumé distribution, follow-up, and evaluation.**
>
> ❑ **"Effectiveness" must include distribution and follow-up— the keys to getting résumés read and responded to.**

Résumé Approaches

Résumé books tend to fall into two general categories—those that primarily emphasize the writing **process** versus those that primarily present **examples**. Most of the process books only address principles of résumé writing and production. A few books, such as this one, attempt to **link** the complete process to the examples as well as to the larger job search process. To our surprise, hardly any books address the critical issues of résumé distribution, follow-up, and evaluation. This seems strange especially when a book claims to offer examples of "effective résumés." After all, "effectiveness" is not only a function of writing and production; it must include **distribution and follow-up**—the keys to getting résumés read and responded to.

While we've tried to present a user-friendly book oriented towards results, we recognize that *Dynamite Résumés* may not answer all of your questions. Therefore, you may want to examine some other résumé books for additional advice and examples. Be forewarned, however, that most of these books primarily focus on writing and production—not distribution, follow-up, and evaluation—and many exhibit the limitations we just discussed. We have found the following books to be some of the better résumé guides available today. Some are available in your local library or bookstore. Most are available directly from the publishers or they can be ordered from Impact Publications.

Adams Media, *Adams Electronic Job Search Almanac 1998* (Holbrook, MA: Adams Media, 1998)

Adams Media (ed.), *The Adams Résumé Almanac* (Holbrook, MA: Adams Media, 1998)

Asher, Donald, *Asher's Bible of Executive Résumés* (Berkeley, CA: Ten Speed Press, 1996)

Asher, Donald, *The Overnight Résumé* (Berkeley, CA: Ten Speed Press, 1991)

Beatty, Richard H., *175 High-Impact Résumés* (New York: Wiley & Sons, 1996)

Beatty, Richard H., *The Résumé Kit* (New York: Wiley & Sons, 1997)

Block, Jay and Michael Betrus, *101 Best Résumés* (New York: McGraw-Hill, 1997)

Career Press (eds.), *101 Great Résumés* (Hawthorne, NJ: Career Press, 1996)

Criscito, Pat, *Résumés in Cyberspace* (New York: Barrons, 1997)

Criscito, Pat, *Designing the Perfect Résumé* (New York: Barrons, 1995)

Career Press (eds.), *Résumés, Résumés, Résumés* (Hawthorne, NJ: Career Press, 1992)

Cochran, Chuck and Donna Peerce, *Heart & Soul Résumés* (Palo Alto, CA: Davies-Black Publishing, 1998)

Cochran, Chuck and Donna Peerce, *Heart & Soul Internet Job Search* (Palo Alto, CA: Davies-Black Publishing, 1999)

Cobin, Bill and Sheby Wright, *The Edge Résumé and Job Search Strategy* (Indianapolis, IN: JIST Works, 1996)

Cowen, Leonard, *Your Résumé: Key to a Better Job, With Disk* (New York: ARCO/Prentice-Hall, 1997)

Enelow, Wendy S., *100 Winning Résumés For $100,000+ Jobs* (Manassas Park, VA: Impact Publications, 1997)

Enelow, Wendy S., *1500+ KeyWords For $100,000+ Jobs* (Manassas Park, VA: Impact Publications, 1998)

Enelow, Wendy S., *Résumé Winners From the Pros* (Manassas Park, VA: Impact Publications, 1998)

Farr, Michael J., *America's Top Résumés For America's Top Jobs* (Indianapolis, IN: JIST Works, 1998)

Farr, Michael J., *The Quick Résumé and Cover Letter Book* (Indianapolis, IN: JIST Works, Inc., 1998)

Fournier, Myra and Jeffrey Spin, *The Encyclopedia of Job-Winning Résumés* (Ridgefield, CT: Round Lake Publishing, 1993)

Gonyea, James C., *Electronic Résumés: Putting Your Résumé On-Line* (New York: McGraw-Hill, 1996)

Good, G. Edward, *Résumés For Re-Entry: A Handbook for Women* (Manassas Park, VA: Impact Publications, 1993)

Ireland, Susan, *The Complete Idiot's Guide to Writing the Perfect Résumé* (New York: Alpha Books, 1997)

Jackson, Tom, *The New Perfect Résumé* (New York: Doubleday, 1996)

Jackson, Tom and Ellen Jackson, *Perfect Résumé Strategies* (New York: Doubleday, 1992)

Jandt, Fred E. and Mary B. Nemnich, *Cyberspace Resume Kit* (Indianapolis, IN: JIST Works, 1998)

Jandt, Fred E. and Mary B. Nemnich, *Using the Internet and the World Wide Web in Your Job Search* (Indianapolis, IN: JIST Works, 1997)

Kaplan, Robbie Miller, *101 Résumés For Sure-Hire Results* (New York: American Management Association, 1994)

Kaplan, Robbie Miller, *Résumé Shortcuts* (Manassas Park, VA: Impact Publications, 1997)

Kaplan, Robbie Miller, *Sure-Hire Résumés* (Manassas Park, VA: Impact Publications, 1998)

Kay, Andrea, *Résumés That Will Get You the Job You Want* (Cincinnati, OH: Betterway Books, 1997)

Kennedy, Joyce Lain and Thomas J. Morrow, *Electronic Résumé Revolution* (New York: Wiley & Sons, 1996)

Kennedy, Joyce Lain, *Résumés For Dummies* (Forest City, CA: IDG Books Worldwide, 1998)

Kimeldorf, Martin, *Portfolio Power* (Princeton, NJ: Peterson's, 1997)

Krannich, Ronald L. and William J. Banis, *High Impact Résumés and Letters* (Manassas Park, VA: Impact Publications, 1998)

Krannich, Ronald L. and Carl S. Savino, *Résumés and Job Search Letters For Transitioning Military Personnel* (Manassas Park, VA: Impact Publications, 1997)

Marino, Kim, *Just Résumés* (New York: Wiley & Sons, 1997)

Montag, Bill, *Best Résumés For $75,000+ Executive Jobs* (New York: Wiley & Sons, 1992)

National Business Employment Weekly, *NBEW's Résumés* (New York: Wiley & Sons, 1996)

Noble, David F., *Gallery of Best Résumés* (Indianapolis, IN: JIST Works, 1994)

Noble, David F., *Gallery of Best Résumés For Two-Year Degree Graduates* (Indianapolis, IN: JIST Works, 1996)

Noble, David F., *Professional Résumés* (Indianapolis, IN: JIST Works, 1998)

Parker, Yana, *Blue Collar and Beyond* (Berkeley, CA: Ten Speed Press, 1994)

Parker, Yana, *The Damn Good Résumé Guide* (Berkeley, CA: Ten Speed Press, 1996)

Parker, Yana, *The Résumé Catalog: 200 Damn Good Examples* (Berkeley, CA: Ten Speed Press, 1988)

Parker, Yana, *The Résumé Pro* (Berkeley, CA: Ten Speed Press, 1992)

Schmidt, Peggy, *The New 90-Minute Résumé, With Software* (Princeton, NJ; Peterson's, 1996)

Swanson, David, *The Résumé Solution: How to Write a Résumé That Gets Results* (Indianapolis, IN: JIST Works, 1995)

Tepper, Ron, *Power Résumés* (New York: Wiley & Sons, 1992)

Troutman, Kathryn K., *The Federal Résumé Guidebook* (Indianapolis, IN: JIST Works, 1997)

Weddle, Peter D., *Internet Résumés* (Manassas Park, VA: Impact Publications, 1998)

Wendleton, Kate, *Building a Great Résumé* (New York: Five O'clock Books, 1997)

Whitcomb, Susan Britton, *Résumé Magic* (Indianapolis, IN: JIST Works, 1998)

Yate, Martin, *Résumés That Knock 'Em Dead* (Holbrook, MA: Adams Media, 1998)

Computer Software Programs

While you can easily produce a résumé on standard word processing programs, such as WordPerfect or Word, several computer software programs are now specially designed for generating résumés in different formats. All you need to do is enter your data for each information category, and the program will do the rest. Keep in mind that these programs will not write the résumé for you. You still need to know how to write each section of your résumé. They merely make the layout and data management tasks easier. They are designed to produce a professional looking résumé.

You will find numerous résumé software programs available at your local computer software store or through direct-mail catalogs. Some programs are not much better than a standard word processing program whereas others are powerful résumé building tools, complete with "canned" résumé language and cover letter capabilities. Some of the best include:

Adams Media (ed.), *The Adams Résumé Almanac With Disk* (Holbrook, MA: Adams Media, 1996)

The Perfect Résumé Computer Kit (Woodstock, NJ: Equinox Interactive/Permax Systems, Inc., 1992)

Parker, Yana, *Ready-to-Go Résumés: Self-Teaching Résumé Templates* (Berkeley, CA: Ten Speed Press, 1994)

The Résumé Kit (Cambridge, MA: Spinnaker Software)

The Right Résumé Writer (Vancouver, WA: The School Company, 1992)

CD-ROMs

More and more résumé programs are now available on CD-ROM. In fact, within the next two years CD-ROMs will probably displace most of the résumé computer software programs. Many CD-ROM programs tend to include video segments and contact managers. Here's what's currently available:

Adams Job Bank CD-ROM (Holbrook, MA: Adams Media)

RésuméMaker CD Deluxe (San Carlos, CA: Individual Software, Inc.)

The Résumé Express (Charleston, WV: Cambridge Career Products)

Win Way Résumés 4.0 (Sacramento, CA: Win-Way Corporation)

The Ultimate Job Source (Orem, UT: InfoBusiness)

Résumé Videos

Several videos also assist résumé writers in developing effective résumé writing skills. Eight such programs include:

Does Your Résumé Wear Blue Jeans? Résumé Writing Workshop (Charlottesville, VA: Blue Jeans Press)

Effective Résumés (Charleston, WV: Cambridge Career Products)

The Ideal Résumé (Charleston, WV: Cambridge Career Products)

The Miracle Résumé (Indianapolis, IN: JIST Works)

The Résumé Remedy (Indianapolis, IN: JIST Works)

The Résumé Zone (Indianapolis, IN: JIST Works)

Ten Commandments of Résumés (Charleston, WV: Cambridge Career Products)

The Video Résumé Writer (Vancouver, WA: The School Company)

Web Résumés (Charleston, WV: Cambridge Career Products)

Résumés For the Rest of Your Worklife

As you'll quickly discover, there are hundreds of resources available to help you write a résumé, including professional résumé writers who will be more than happy to write your résumé for $100 to $300. Sorting through all the conflicting advice and examples can be a daunting task, especially if you need to quickly put together a résumé. If you follow our advice, you should be able to write, produce, and distribute your own dynamite résumé and continue doing so with impact the rest of your worklife.

9

Résumé Worksheets

The following worksheets are designed to help you systematically generate a complete database on yourself for writing each résumé section. We recommend completing the forms **before** writing your résumé.

Generate the Right Data On Yourself

You will be in the strongest position to write each résumé section after you document, analyze, and synthesize different types of data on yourself based on these forms. Each form will assist you in specifying your accomplishments and generating the proper résumé language. Since you are likely to have more experience/education than the number of worksheets provided here, make several copies of these worksheets if necessary to complete the exercises.

Try to complete each form as thoroughly as possible. While you will not include all the information on your résumé, you will at least have a rich database from which to write each résumé section. Our general rule is to go for volume—generate as much detailed information on yourself as possible. Condense it later when writing and editing each résumé section.

The final worksheet focuses on detailing your **achievements**. In many respects, this may be the most important worksheet of all. After you complete the other worksheets, try to identify your seven most important achievements. The language generated here will be important to both writing your résumé and handling the critical job interview. You should be well prepared to clearly communicate your qualifications to potential employers!

Employment Experience Worksheet

1. Name of employer: _____

2. Address: _____

   _____

3. Inclusive dates of employment: From _____ to _____.
   month/year   month/year

4. Type of organization: _____

5. Size of organization/approximate number of employees: _____

6. Approximate annual sales volume or annual budget: _____

7. Position held: _____

8. Earnings per month/year: (not to appear on résumé) _____

9. Responsibilities/duties: _____

   _____

   _____

   _____

10. Achievements or significant contributions: _____

    _____

    _____

    _____

    _____

11. Demonstrated skills and abilities: _____

    _____

    _____

12. Reason(s) for leaving: _____

    _____

Military Experience Worksheet

1. Service: _____

2. Rank: _____

3. Inclusive dates: From _____ to _____.
                       month/year   month/year

4. Responsibilities/duties: _____

   _____

   _____

   _____

   _____

5. Significant contributions/achievements: _____

   _____

   _____

   _____

   _____

   _____

6. Demonstrated skills and abilities: _____

   _____

   _____

   _____

   _____

   _____

7. Reserve status: _____

Educational Data

1. Institution: _____

2. Address: _____

   _____

3. Inclusive dates: From _____ to _____.
                      month/year   month/year

4. Degree or years completed: _____

5. Major(s): _____ Minor(s): _____

6. Education highlights: _____

   _____

   _____

7. Student activities: _____

   _____

   _____

8. Demonstrated abilities and skills: _____

   _____

   _____

9. Significant contributions/achievements: _____

   _____

   _____

10. Special training courses: _____

    _____

    _____

11. G.P.A.: _____ (on _____ index)

Community/Civic/
Volunteer Experience

1. Name and address of organization/group: _____

_____

_____

2. Inclusive dates: From _____ to _____.
   month/year   month/year

3. Offices held/nature of involvement: _____

_____

_____

_____

_____

4. Significant contributions/achievements/projects: _____

_____

_____

_____

_____

_____

5. Demonstrated skills and abilities: _____

_____

_____

_____

_____

_____

Additional Information

1. Professional memberships and status:

   a. _____

   b. _____

   c. _____

   d. _____

2. Licenses/certifications:

   a. _____

   b. _____

   c. _____

   d. _____

3. Expected salary range: $ _____ to $ _____ (do not include on résumé)

4. Acceptable amount of on-the-job travel: _____ days per month.

5. Areas of acceptable relocation:

   a. _____   c. _____

   b. _____   d. _____

6. Date of availability: _____

7. Contacting present employer:

   a. Is he or she aware of your prospective job change? _____

   b. May he or she be contacted at this time? _____

8. References: (name, address, telephone number—not to appear on résumé)

   a. _____   b. _____

      _____   _____

      _____   _____

   c. _____   d. _____

      _____   _____

      _____   _____

9. Foreign languages and degree of competency:

    a. _____

    b. _____

10. Interests and activities: hobbies, avocations, pursuits

    a. _____

    b. _____

    c. _____

    d. _____

Circle letter of ones which support your objective.

11. Foreign travel:

	Country	Purpose	Dates
a.	_____	_____	_____
b.	_____	_____	_____
c.	_____	_____	_____
d.	_____	_____	_____
e.	_____	_____	_____

12. Special awards/recognition:

    a. _____

    b. _____

    c. _____

    d. _____

13. Special abilities/skills/talents/accomplishments:

    a. _____

    b. _____

    c. _____

    d. _____

Detail Your Achievements

Definition: An "Achievement" is anything you enjoyed doing, believe you did well, and felt a sense of satisfaction, pride, or accomplishment in doing.

ACHIEVEMENT # _____: _____

_____

1. How did I initially become involved? _____

_____

_____

_____

2. What did I do? _____

_____

_____

_____

3. How did I do it? _____

_____

_____

_____

_____

4. What was especially enjoyable about doing it? _____

_____

_____

_____

_____

The Authors

Ronald L. Krannich, Ph.D. and Caryl Rae Krannich, Ph.D., are two of America's leading business and travel writers who have authored more than 40 books. They currently operate Development Concepts Inc., a training, consulting, and publishing firm. A former Peace Corps Volunteer and Fulbright Scholar, Ron received his Ph.D. in Political Science from Northern Illinois University. Caryl received her Ph.D. in Speech Communication from Penn State University.

Ron and Caryl are former university professors, high school teachers, management trainers, and consultants. As trainers and consultants, they have completed numerous projects on management, career development, local government, population planning, and rural development in the United States and abroad.

The Krannichs' business and career work encompasses nearly 30 books they have authored on a variety of subjects: key job search skills, public speaking, government jobs, international careers, nonprofit organizations, and career transitions. Their work represents one of today's most extensive and highly praised collections of career and business writing: *101 Dynamite Answers to Interview Questions, 101 Secrets of Highly Effective Speakers, 201 Dynamite Job Search Letters, The Best Jobs For the 21st Century, Change Your Job Change Your Life, The Complete Guide to International Jobs and Careers,*

182

Discover the Best Jobs For You, Dynamite Cover Letters, Dynamite Résumés, Dynamite Salary Negotiations, Dynamite Tele-Search, The Educator's Guide to Alternative Jobs and Careers, Find a Federal Job Fast, From Air Force Blue to Corporate Gray, From Army Green to Corporate Gray, From Navy Blue to Corporate Gray, Résumés and Job Search Letters For Transitioning Military Personnel, High Impact Résumés and Letters, International Jobs Directory, Interview For Success, Jobs and Careers With Nonprofit Organizations, Jobs For People Who Love Travel, Get a Raise in 7 Days, and *Dynamite Networking For Dynamite Jobs*. Their books are found in most major bookstores, libraries, and career centers as well as on Impact's Web site: *www.impactpublications.com*. Many of their works are available interactively on CD-ROM (*The Ultimate Job Source*).

Ron and Caryl live a double career life. Authors of 13 travel books, the Krannichs continue to pursue their international interests through their innovative and highly acclaimed Impact Guides travel series (*"The Treasures and Pleasures....Best of the Best"*) which currently encompasses separate titles on Italy, France, China, Hong Kong, Thailand, Indonesia, Singapore, Malaysia, India, and Australia. When not found at their home and business in Virginia, they are probably somewhere in Europe, Asia, Africa, the Middle East, the South Pacific, or the Caribbean pursuing one of their major passions—researching and writing about quality arts and antiques.

The Krannichs reside in Northern Virginia. Frequent speakers and seminar leaders, they can be contacted through the publisher or by e-mail:

krannich@impactpublications.com

Index

Career Resources

Contact Impact Publications for a free annotated listing of career resources or visit their World Wide Web site for a complete listing of career resources: ***www.impactpublications.com***

The following career resources, many of which were mentioned in previous chapters, are available directly from Impact Publications. Complete the following form or list the titles, include postage (see formula at the end), enclose payment, and send your order to:

IMPACT PUBLICATIONS
9104-N Manassas Drive
Manassas Park, VA 20111-5211
1-800-361-1055 (orders only)
Tel. 703/361-7300 or Fax 703/335-9486
E-mail: *resume@impactpublications.com*

Orders from individuals must be prepaid by check, moneyorder, Visa, MasterCard, or American Express. We accept telephone and fax orders.

Qty.	TITLES	Price	TOTAL

Job Search Strategies and Tactics

Qty.	TITLES	Price	TOTAL
___	Career Chase	$17.95	___
___	Change Your Job, Change Your Life	17.95	___
___	Complete Idiot's Guide to Getting the Job You Want	24.95	___
___	Complete Job Finder's Guide to the 90's	13.95	___
___	Five Secrets to Finding a Job	12.95	___
___	How to Get Interviews From Classified Job Ads	14.95	___
___	How to Succeed Without a Career Path	13.95	___
___	Me, Myself, and I, Inc	17.95	___

___	New Rites of Passage at $100,000+	29.95	___
___	The Pathfinder	14.00	___
___	What Color Is Your Parachute?	16.95	___
___	Who's Running Your Career	14.95	___

Best Jobs and Employers For the 21st Century

___	50 Coolest Jobs in Sports	15.95	___
___	100 Best Careers For the 21st Century	15.95	___
___	100 Jobs in the Environment	14.95	___
___	100 Jobs in Technology	14.95	___
___	Adams Jobs Almanac 1998	15.95	___
___	American Almanac of Jobs and Salaries	20.00	___
___	Best Jobs For the 21st Century	19.95	___
___	Breaking and Entering: Jobs in Film Production	17.95	___
___	Careers Encyclopedia	39.95	___
___	Cool Careers For Dummies	19.99	___
___	Great Jobs Ahead	11.95	___
___	Jobs 1999	15.00	___
___	Jobs Rated Almanac	16.95	___
___	Sunshine Jobs	16.95	___
___	The Top 100	19.95	___

Key Directories

___	American Salaries and Wages Survey	110.00	___
___	Business Phone Book USA 1999	160.00	___
___	Careers Encyclopedia	39.95	___
___	Complete Guide to Occupational Exploration	39.95	___
___	Consultants & Consulting Organizations Directory 1999	605.00	___
___	Dictionary of Occupational Titles	47.95	___
___	Encyclopedia of American Industries 1998	520.00	___
___	Encyclopedia of Associations 1999 (all 3 volumes)	1260.00	___
___	Encyclopedia of Associations 1999 (National only)	490.00	___
___	Encyclopedia of Careers & Vocational Guidance	149.95	___
___	Enhanced Guide For Occupational Exploration	34.95	___
___	Enhanced Occupational Outlook Handbook	34.95	___
___	Job Hunter's Sourcebook	70.00	___
___	National Job Bank 1999	350.00	___
___	National Job Hotline Directory	16.95	___
___	National Trade & Professional Associations 1998	129.00	___
___	Occupational Outlook Handbook, 1998-99	22.95	___
___	O*NET Dictionary of Occupational Titles	49.95	___
___	Professional Careers Sourcebook	99.00	___
___	Specialty Occupational Outlook: Professions	49.95	___
___	Specialty Occupational Outlook: Trade & Technical	49.95	___
___	Vocational Careers Sourcebook	82.00	___

Education Directories

___	Free and Inexpensive Career Materials	19.95	___
___	Internships 1999	24.95	___
___	Peterson's Guide to Graduate & Professional Programs	239.95	___

___	Peterson's Two- and Four-Year Colleges 1999	45.95 ___
___	Scholarships, Fellowships, & Loans 1999	165.00 ___

Electronic Job Search

___	Adams Electronic Job Search Almanac 1998	9.95 ___
___	Career Exploration On the Internet	15.95 ___
___	CareerXroads 1998	22.95 ___
___	Cyberspace Resume Kit	16.95 ___
___	Guide to Internet Job Search	14.95 ___
___	How to Get Your Dream Job Using the Web	29.99 ___
___	Internet Resumes	14.95 ___
___	Job Searching Online For Dummies	24.99 ___
___	Using the Internet and the WWW in Your Job Search	16.95 ___

Best Companies

___	Hidden Job Market 1999	18.95 ___
___	Hoover's Top 2,500 Employers	22.95 ___
___	Job Vault	20.00 ___
___	JobBank Guide to Computer & High-Tech Companies	16.95 ___
___	JobBank Guide to Health Care Companies	16.95 ___

$100,000+ Jobs

___	$100,000 Club	25.00 ___
___	$100,000 Resume	16.95 ___
___	100 Winning Resumes For $100,000+ Jobs	24.95 ___
___	201 Winning Cover Letters For $100,000+ Jobs	24.95 ___
___	1500+ KeyWords For $100,000+ Jobs	14.95 ___
___	New Rites of Passage at $100,000+	29.95 ___
___	Six-Figure Consulting	17.95 ___
___	Winning Interviews For $100,000+ Jobs	14.95 ___

Finding Great Jobs

___	5 O'Clock Club Job Search Skills Program	43.95 ___
___	100 Best Careers in Casinos and Casino Hotels	15.95 ___
___	101 Ways to Power Up Your Job Search	12.95 ___
___	110 Biggest Mistakes Job Hunters Make	19.95 ___
___	Adams Executive Recruiters Almanac	16.95 ___
___	Alternative Careers in Secret Operations	19.95 ___
___	Back Door Guide to Short-Term Job Adventures	19.95 ___
___	Careers For College Majors	32.95 ___
___	College Grad Job Hunter	14.95 ___
___	Directory of Executive Recruiters 1999	44.95 ___
___	First Job Hunt Survival Guide	11.95 ___
___	Get Ahead! Stay Ahead!	12.95 ___
___	Get a Job You Love!	19.95 ___
___	Get What You Deserve!	23.00 ___
___	Great Jobs For Liberal Arts Majors	11.95 ___
___	How to Get Interviews From Classified Job Ads	14.95 ___
___	In Transition	12.50 ___
___	Job Hunting Made Easy	12.95 ___

___	Job Search: The Total System	14.95	___
___	Job Search 101	12.95	___
___	Job Seekers Guide to Executive Recruiters	34.95	___
___	Job Search Organizer	12.95	___
___	Jobs & Careers With Nonprofit Organizations	15.95	___
___	JobSmart	12.00	___
___	Knock 'Em Dead	12.95	___
___	New Relocating Spouse's Guide to Employment	14.95	___
___	No One Is Unemployable	29.95	___
___	Non-Profits and Education Job Finder	16.95	___
___	Perfect Pitch	13.99	___
___	Professional's Job Finder	18.95	___
___	Strategic Job Jumping	20.00	___
___	Top Career Strategies For the Year 2000 & Beyond	12.00	___
___	What Do I Say Next?	20.00	___
___	What Employers Really Want.	14.95	___
___	Work Happy Live Healthy	14.95	___
___	World Almanac Job Finder's Guide	24.95	___
___	You Can't Play the Game If You Don't Know the Rules	14.95	___

Assessment

___	Discover the Best Jobs For You	14.95	___
___	Discover What You're Best At	12.00	___
___	Do What You Are	16.95	___
___	Finding Your Perfect Work	16.95	___
___	I Could Do Anything If Only I Knew What It Was	19.95	___
___	Richard Bolles Self-Assessment Tool Kit	19.95	___

Inspiration & Empowerment

___	100 Ways to Motivate Yourself	15.99	___
___	Career Busters	10.95	___
___	Chicken Soup For the Soul Series	75.95	___
___	Doing Work You Love	14.95	___
___	Emotional Intelligence	13.95	___
___	Personal Job Power	12.95	___
___	Power of Purpose	20.00	___
___	Seven Habits of Highly Effective People	14.00	___
___	Survival Personality	12.00	___
___	To Build the Life You Want, Create the Work You Love	10.95	___
___	Your Signature Path	24.95	___

Resumes

___	100 Winning Resumes For $100,000+ Jobs	24.95	___
___	101 Best Resumes	10.95	___
___	1500+ KeyWords For $100,000+ Jobs	14.95	___
___	$100,000 Resume	16.95	___
___	Adams Resumes Almanac & Disk	19.95	___
___	America's Top Resumes For America's Top Jobs	19.95	___
___	Asher's Bible of Executive Resumes	29.95	___
___	Best Resumes For $75,000+ Executive Jobs	14.95	___
___	Better Resumes in Three Easy Steps	12.95	___

___	Complete Idiot's Guide to Writing the Perfect Resume	16.95 ___
___	Designing the Perfect Resume	12.95 ___
___	Dynamite Resumes	14.95 ___
___	Encyclopedia of Job-Winning Resumes	16.95 ___
___	Gallery of Best Resumes	16.95 ___
___	Gallery of Best Resumes For Two-Year Degree Grads	14.95 ___
___	Heart and Soul Resumes	15.95 ___
___	High Impact Resumes & Letters	19.95 ___
___	How to Prepare Your Curriculum Vitae	14.95 ___
___	Internet Resumes	14.95 ___
___	Just Resumes	11.95 ___
___	New 90-Minute Resumes	15.95 ___
___	New Perfect Resume	12.00 ___
___	Portfolio Power	14.95 ___
___	Ready-to-Go Resumes	29.95 ___
___	Resume Catalog	15.95 ___
___	Resume Shortcuts	14.95 ___
___	Resumes & Job Search Letters For Transitioning Military Personnel	17.95 ___
___	Resumes For Dummies	12.99 ___
___	Resumes For Re-Entry	10.95 ___
___	Resumes in Cyberspace	14.95 ___
___	Resumes That Knock 'Em Dead	14.95 ___
___	Sure-Hire Resumes	14.95 ___

Cover Letters

___	175 High-Impact Cover Letters	10.95 ___
___	201 Dynamite Job Search Letters	19.95 ___
___	201 Killer Cover Letters	16.95 ___
___	201 Winning Cover Letters For $100,000+ Jobs	24.95 ___
___	Adams Cover Letter Almanac & Disk	19.95 ___
___	Complete Idiot's Guide to the Perfect Cover Letter	14.95 ___
___	Cover Letters For Dummies	12.99 ___
___	Cover Letters That Knock 'Em Dead	10.95 ___
___	Dynamite Cover Letters	14.95 ___

Networking

___	Dynamite Networking For Dynamite Jobs	15.95 ___
___	Dynamite Telesearch	12.95 ___
___	Great Connections	19.95 ___
___	How to Work a Room	11.99 ___
___	People Power	14.95 ___
___	Power Networking	14.95 ___
___	Power Schmoozing	12.95 ___
___	Power to Get In	24.95 ___

Interview & Communication Skills

___	90-Minute Interview Prep Book	15.95 ___
___	101 Dynamite Answers to Interview Questions	12.95 ___
___	101 Dynamite Questions to Ask At Your Job Interview	14.95 ___
___	101 Great Answers to the Toughest Interview Questions	9.99 ___

___	101 Secrets of Highly Effective Speakers	14.95 ___
___	111 Dynamite Ways to Ace Your Job Interview	13.95 ___
___	Complete Idiot's Guide to the Perfect Job Interview	14.95 ___
___	Complete Q & A Job Interview Book	14.95 ___
___	Interview For Success	15.95 ___
___	Interview Power	12.95 ___
___	Job Interviews For Dummies	12.99 ___
___	Winning Interviews For $100,000+ Jobs	14.95 ___

Salary Negotiations

___	Dynamite Salary Negotiations	15.95 ___
___	Get More Money On Your Next Job	14.95 ___
___	Get a Raise in 7 Days	14.95 ___
___	Negotiate Your Job Offer	14.95 ___

Government & Law Enforcement Jobs

___	Barron's Guide to Law Enforcement Careers	13.95 ___
___	Complete Guide to Public Employment	19.95 ___
___	Directory of Federal Jobs and Employers	21.95 ___
___	Federal Applications That Get Results	23.95 ___
___	Federal Jobs in Law Enforcement	14.95 ___
___	Find a Federal Job Fast!	15.95 ___
___	Government Job Finder	16.95 ___
___	Jobs For Lawyers	14.95 ___
___	Paralegal Career Guide	24.95 ___
___	Post Office Jobs	17.95 ___
___	Quick & Easy Federal Application Kit	49.95 ___

International & Travel

___	Complete Guide to International Jobs & Careers	24.95 ___
___	Great Jobs Abroad	14.95 ___
___	International Jobs Directory	19.95 ___
___	Jobs For People Who Love Travel	15.95 ___
___	Jobs in Paradise	14.95 ___
___	Jobs In Russia & the Newly Independent States	15.95 ___
___	Jobs Worldwide	17.95 ___

CD-ROMs

___	Adams Job Bank CD-ROM	49.95 ___
___	RésuméMaker CD-ROM Deluxe	59.95 ___
___	Résumé Express	99.00 ___
___	Ultimate Job Source CD-ROM	49.95 ___
___	What Color Is Your Parachute CD-ROM	49.95 ___
___	Win Way Résumés 4.0	49.95 ___

Videos

___	Does Your Résumé Wear Blue Jeans? Video Workshop	99.95 ___
___	Effective Résumés	98.00 ___

___	Ideal Résumé	79.95	_____
___	Miracle Résumé	119.00	_____
___	Résumé Remedy	139.00	_____
___	Résumé Zone	129.00	_____
___	Ten Commandments of Résumés	79.95	_____
___	Ten Ways to Get a Great Job	79.95	_____
___	Tough New Labor Market...	195.00	_____
___	Understanding/Using O*NET	119.00	_____
___	Why Should I Hire You?	129.00	_____
___	You're Hired!	129.00	_____

SUBTOTAL   _____

Virginia residents add 4½% sales tax   _____

POSTAGE/HANDLING ($5 for first
product and 8% of SUBTOTAL over $30) $5.00

8% of SUBTOTAL over $30 ------------------------------------- _____

TOTAL ENCLOSED ------------------------------------- _____

NAME _____

ADDRESS _____

_____

_____

❑ I enclose check/moneyorder for $ _____ made payable to
    IMPACT PUBLICATIONS.

❑ Please charge $ _____ to my credit card:
    ❑ Visa   ❑ MasterCard   ❑ American Express   ❑ Discover

    Card # _____

    Expiration date: _____/_____ Tel. _____/_____

    Signature _____

Your One-Stop Online Superstore

Hundreds of Terrific Resources Conveniently Available On the World Wide Web 24-Hours a Day, 365 Days a Year!

Ever wanted to know what are the newest and best books, directories, newsletters, wall charts, training programs, videos, CD-ROMs, computer software, and kits available to help you land a job, negotiate a higher salary, or start your own business? What about finding a job in Asia or relocating to San Francisco? Are you curious about how to find a job 24-hours a day by using the Internet or what you'll be doing five years from now? Trying to keep up-to-date on the latest career resources but not able to find the latest catalogs, brochures, or newsletters on today's "best of the best" resources?

Welcome to the first virtual career bookstore on the Internet. Now you're only a "click" away with Impact Publication's electronic solution to the resource challenge. Impact Publications, one of the nation's leading publishers and distributors of career resources, offers the most comprehensive "Career Superstore and Warehouse" on the Internet. The bookstore is jam-packed with the latest job and career resources on:

- Alternative jobs and careers
- Self-assessment
- Career planning and job search
- Employers
- Relocation and cities
- Resumes
- Cover Letters
- Dress, image, and etiquette
- Education
- Recruitment
- Military
- Salaries
- Interviewing
- Nonprofits

- Empowerment
- Self-esteem
- Goal setting
- Executive recruiters
- Entrepreneurship
- Government
- Networking
- Electronic job search
- International jobs
- Travel
- Law
- Training and presentations
- Minorities
- Physically challenged

The bookstore also includes sections for ex-offenders and middle schools.

"This is more than just a bookstore offering lots of product," say Drs. Ron and Caryl Krannich, two of the nation's leading career experts and authors and developers of this on-line bookstore. *"We're an important resource center for libraries, corporations, government, educators, trainers, and career counselors who are constantly defining and redefining this dynamic field. Of the thousands of career resources we review each year, we only select the 'best of the best.'"*

Visit this rich site and you'll quickly discover just about everything you ever wanted to know about finding jobs, changing careers, and starting your own business—including many useful resources that are difficult to find in local bookstores and libraries. The site also includes tips for job search success and monthly specials. Its shopping cart and special search feature make this one of the most convenient Web sites to use. Impact's Internet address is:

www.impactpublications.com